OVERLORD

– 6 JUNE 1944 –

OVERLORD
– 6 JUNE 1944 –
D-DAY AND THE BATTLE FOR NORMANDY

THE PAINTINGS OF THE MILITARY GALLERY

GRIFFON INTERNATIONAL

OVERLORD
6 JUNE 1944
D-DAY AND THE BATTLE FOR NORMANDY

THE PAINTINGS OF THE MILITARY GALLERY

ISBN 978-0-9549970-3-8
A GRIFFON INTERNATIONAL BOOK

First published in the United Kingdom in 2014 by Griffon International Limited,
2 Station Approach, Wendover, Buckinghamshire, HP22 6BN

A catalogue record for this book is available from the British Library.

Printed in China
Design and typesetting by Ingrid Freeman.
Created and written by Michael Craig.

CONTENTS

PART ONE – INVASION

CONTENTS

CONTENTS

PART TWO – WINGS OF VICTORY

HELL HAWKS OVER THE NORMANDY BRIDGEHEAD by Robert Taylor

FOREWORD

The compilation of drawings and paintings illustrated in this new volume has been assembled from the archives of the Military Gallery. Together with work specially commissioned for this new book, they form the backbone of an unrivalled anthology of artistic work depicting the events of D-Day and the subsequent battle for Normandy.

The Military Gallery was established in 1975, and has been credited with creating the genre of outstanding images published as limited edition prints autographed by the veterans who served us so heroically during World War II. Many of the most iconic paintings of this genre have come from the Military Gallery who continue to inspire us with this new book published to commemorate the 70th Anniversary of the D-Day landings in Normandy.

The paintings and drawings in the book are the work of five talented artists who, through their work, help to impart some of the emotion that photographs so often fail to capture:

Robert Taylor, widely acknowledged as the world's premier aviation and maritime artist, leads the way. Who can fail to be moved by his painting *D-Day - The Airborne Assault*, the depiction of C-47s, closely escorted by P-51 Mustangs, towing CG-4A Waco gliders carrying the daytime lift of American airborne troops as they pass over the invasion beaches?

The paintings of Anthony Saunders and Chris Collingwood, two of the most inspirational artists of their generation, help us to follow the timeline of events that took place in June 1944; as do those of Simon Smith, who is equally at home painting in traditional oils or using digital technologies to create stunning D-Day images.

The majority of pencil drawings in this eye-catching book come from the studio of Richard Taylor, who has undoubtedly inherited his father's artistic talent. Skilfully executed with a flair that belies his age, these exceptional works help knit together this brief account of D-Day, and turn it into a visual masterpiece.

FOUR YEARS TO THE DAY

DUNKIRK: 4 JUNE 1940

'A colossal military failure' Winston Churchill

4 June 1940, and as dawn broke over the dull grey waters of the Channel the last weary troops of what had been the British Expeditionary Force were evacuated from the blood-stained sands of Dunkirk. Nearly 220,000 British and 120,000 French and Belgian soldiers had miraculously been lifted to safety by a hastily improvised fleet that included paddle steamers, lifeboats, fishing boats and pleasure craft, the famous 'little ships'. Left behind, however, was the debris of a broken and shattered army.

Yet Dunkirk wasn't quite the end. Over the next three weeks the retreat of those Allied fighting forces that still existed in France - including the British 51st (Highland) Division and the 1st Armoured Division who had been fighting further south along the Somme - became a rout. Exhausted men fell back before the onslaught in a brave attempt to reach those ports still in Allied hands - Le Havre, Cherbourg, Brest, St Nazaire, La Palice, Bordeaux and Bayonne. It was a race against time and many didn't make it. On 12 June the battered remnants of the 51st Highland, along with four French divisions, were encircled and forced to surrender at the Channel port of St-Valéry-en-Caux after only a few thousand had been rescued. Le Havre fell the same day.

At Cherbourg the recently arrived 52nd (Lowland) Division, together with the 1st Armoured Division, did manage to escape - just; the last ship embarked the rearguard and was steaming out past the outer breakwater at 'full speed ahead' as the first German units entered the town. It had been a close-run thing. Likewise at St Malo, over 20,000 men of the Canadian 1st Division, also recently arrived, were hastily re-embarked and sailed to safety before the port fell.

It was the same at Brest where over 30,000 troops, many of them RAF ground crew and Army support staff, were evacuated, whilst at St Nazaire others waited patiently on the quays, including battered units of Polish and Czech troops for whom it had been an even longer and more dispiriting journey. As they climbed aboard the ships sent from England, the news that the French government had sought an armistice with the Germans was confirmed. Hostilities were to cease at noon on 25 June. As if to confirm the calamity, the troopship *Lancastria* was sunk by Luftwaffe bombers with the loss of 4,000 men.

In the space of just six weeks the Germans had overrun the west. It had been a humiliating defeat, yet the evacuation from Dunkirk followed by those from the western ports had saved over half a million fighting men. If France were ever to be liberated the Allies would need every one of them, but for now Britain stood alone. *Operation Sealion* - the German invasion of Britain - was imminent.

THE RAF AT DUNKIRK

As the Panzers tightened their stranglehold on Dunkirk, the Luftwaffe did its best to destroy the last remnants of the Allied armies from the air. On the beaches many soldiers bitterly complained 'Where's the RAF?'

The RAF, however, were there, but not always over the beaches. Against the odds they were valiantly trying to intercept the Luftwaffe long before they reached Dunkirk. In a desperate struggle Fighter Command flew over 5,000 combat missions during the Dunkirk evacuation, losing over 100 aircraft. Without the protective screen of fighters provided by the RAF, the casualties suffered during the withdrawal would undoubtedly have been higher. On 29 May Admiral Bertram Ramsey, Flag Officer, Dover in command of *Operation Dynamo* sent a message to Fighter Command: 'I am most grateful for your splendid co-operation,' he said, 'It alone has given us a chance of success…'

Churchill, too, was quick to praise the RAF: 'We must be very careful not to assign to this deliverance the attributes of a victory. Wars are not won by evacuations', he said 'but there was a victory inside this deliverance....it was gained by the Air Force'.

VICTORY OVER DUNKIRK by Robert Taylor

Spitfire 'Ace' Bob Stanford-Tuck in action over Dunkirk on 23 May 1940 as he downs one of three Me110s he destroyed that day.

FOUR YEARS TO THE DAY

PORTSMOUTH: 4 JUNE 1944

"Soldiers, Sailors and Airmen of the Allied Expeditionary Force! You are about to embark upon a great crusade, toward which we have striven these many months. The eyes of the world are upon you. The hopes and prayers of liberty-loving people everywhere march with you". Dwight D. Eisenhower

4 June 1944, and the waters of Portsmouth harbour were black with ships. Vessels of every conceivable shape and size jostled alongside each other, vying for space. Battleships, monitors, cruisers and destroyers towered over minesweepers and landing craft, whilst others embarked tanks, trucks, armoured vehicles and thousands of fighting men weighed down with equipment. Transports, stowed to the gunnels with ammunition and supplies, rode low in the water surrounded by escorts and launches, whilst tugs hustled and bustled amongst throngs of miscellaneous barges, some of which were floating kitchens.

It was a scene by and large replicated in every harbour, large or small, in every sheltered estuary and inlet anchorage along the entire coast of southern England. The largest fleet assembled in the history of mankind stood poised, ready to carry a liberating army across the Channel to Normandy.

Portsmouth was now the headquarters of the Supreme Commander of the Allied Forces in Europe - General Dwight D. Eisenhower - but like many other British cities, it had been in the front line ever since

A detail from **FURY OF ASSAULT** by Robert Taylor

Portsmouth, as with London, Coventry, Liverpool and other major cities, had been heavily bombed by the Luftwaffe.

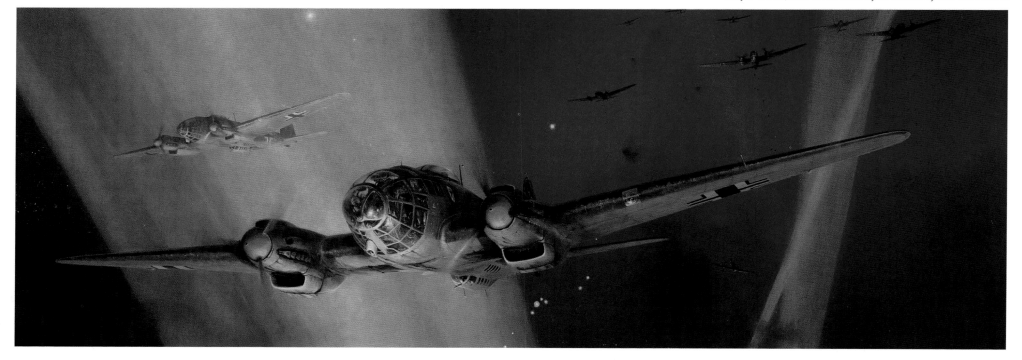

12

Dunkirk. It had witnessed the Battle of Britain when the Spitfire and Hurricane pilots of RAF Fighter Command had defeated the Luftwaffe and exorcised the spectre of a German occupation. Along with London, Coventry, Liverpool, Southampton and others, Portsmouth, with its huge naval dockyard, had been heavily bombed. But then Hitler, thwarted in his attempt to invade Britain, had turned his ravenous gaze eastwards towards Russia as the Italians, under the dictator Benito Mussolini, joined an unholy alliance with Germany. Together, their forces in North Africa advanced menacingly towards Egypt.

As the Battle of Britain was reaching its climax in September 1940, Germany and Italy signed a treaty with Japan. It promised to 'assist one another with all political, economic and military means' when attacked.

AMERICA ENTERS THE WAR

It was also a treaty that would change the course of the war: the day after the unprovoked Japanese attack on the American Pacific fleet at Pearl Harbour on 7 December 1941, and the bombing of Singapore the following day, America and Britain declared war on Japan. Three days later, on 11 December 1941, Germany and Italy in accordance with their treaty, declared war on America. What had been a European war was now a global one.

America, by far the world's most powerful economy, went into overdrive. With seemingly limitless natural resources and a prodigious manufacturing capacity,

American matériel and manpower would transform the war in Europe. An ever-increasing stream of equipment, supplies, fuel and fighting men began to flow relentlessly across the Atlantic into Britain. Few now doubted that France would one day be liberated. The only question was when.

At Portsmouth on 4 June 1944 General Eisenhower stood ready to announce the answer to the question: *Operation Overlord* - the Allied invasion of Normandy - was about to begin.

DAY OF INFAMY by Anthony Saunders

On 7 December 1941 the Japanese launched their infamous, unprovoked attack on the US Pacific Fleet anchored at Pearl Harbor. The war had come to America.

SECRET OPERATION by Robert Taylor

Royal Navy submarines, such as HMS *Sceptre*, were involved in landing raiding parties and clandestine operatives on the shores of France.

PLANNING FOR OVERLORD

Ever since 1942 a small group of military planners, operating from obscure rooms in un-named War Office buildings, had been working on the problem, accumulating information ready for the day when a return to Europe would be possible. At the end of 1943, the decision to invade north-west France the following year - codenamed *Operation Overlord* - was made and Lieutenant General Frederick Morgan was appointed Chief of Staff to the Supreme Allied Commander - or COSSAC. His job was to prepare a blueprint for the invasion and one of the first decisions to make was where?

The planners already had a treasure trove of information: the BBC had broadcast a request for listeners to send in any pre-war postcards, holiday snaps or guidebooks - anything relating to the coast of Europe. Expecting a few thousand, ten million arrived!

Now photo-reconnaissance squadrons were diverted to photograph the French beaches, harbours and coastal defences whilst an increasing number of commando raids across the Channel probed for any weaknesses. Daring clandestine sorties were carried out by frogmen and canoeists from the Combined Operations Pilotage Parties - COPPS - who swam ashore in the dead of night to reconnoitre suitable beaches. The choice of locations was whittled down to three: the Pas de Calais, or the coasts of either Normandy or Brittany.

The first was the obvious choice - the Pas de Calais. It offered the shortest sea crossing, although the ports of Dover and Folkestone from which such an operation might be mounted, were small. The rolling hinterland of the Pas de Calais was well suited to armour - as the British and French had found to their cost in 1940 - and Calais was the nearest point on the French coast to the Ruhr, whose industry supplied a major part of Germany's manufacturing capacity. Dortmund, Duisburg and Essen are all closer to Calais than they are to Berlin.

The Pas de Calais, however, was the obvious choice to the Germans, too: the strength of the defences along the coast here surpassed any other part of Hitler's 'Atlantic Wall' - the defensive line that ran from Denmark to the Bay of Biscay.

An invasion through Brittany was possible, provided its deep water ports were captured intact, but it was the furthest away. Morgan and his team opted instead for the beaches of Normandy and, within three months of his appointment, he submitted his 'COSSAC' plan to the Chiefs of Staff.

The outline plan was agreed, in principle, and a proposed date set - 1 May 1944.

THE 'COSSAC' PLAN:

- An amphibious landing by three divisions on the beaches north of Caen, keeping the beachhead within range of Allied fighter-cover.
- Once the beachhead had been secured, pre-fabricated harbours would be towed across the Channel so that supplies and reinforcements could be landed en-masse, whilst the army moved north to capture the port of Cherbourg.
- Airfields would be constructed on the Cherbourg peninsula.
- Bolstered by the use of Cherbourg the army would then thrust west into Brittany to capture the ports there, and east towards the Seine and Le Havre.

Part of COSSAC included an intricate series of deceptions to lure the Germans into believing that the attack would be elsewhere, the most important being *Operation Fortitude South,* to convince the enemy that the main assault would be in the Pas de Calais. Under the codename *Quicksilver* an entire mythical army, commanded by a very real General George Patton, was created to assist in the deception.

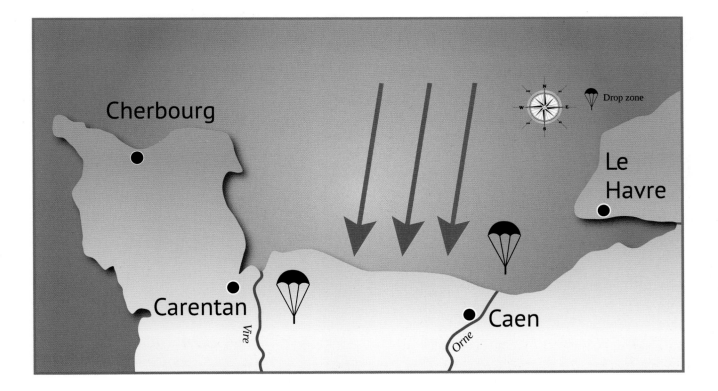

SHAEF
SUPREME HEADQUARTERS ALLIED EXPEDITIONARY FORCE

On 6 December 1943 President Roosevelt appointed the American General, Dwight D. Eisenhower, as Supreme Allied Commander to take over from COSSAC. The United States were to provide more men for *Overlord* than any other nation - by June 1944 more than 1,750,000 American troops were stationed in Britain. Eisenhower's deputy was to be British - Air Chief Marshal Sir Arthur Tedder.

The Allied Naval Commander in charge of *Operation Neptune*, the naval assault phase of *Overlord*, would be Admiral Sir Bertram Ramsey, the hero of Dunkirk, whilst the position of Allied Expeditionary Air Force Commander was given to Air Chief Marshal Sir Trafford Leigh Mallory from the RAF.

On land the 21st Army Group - which consisted of the main American, British and Canadian Armies that would carry out the invasion - was put under the control of General Bernard Montgomery, victor of El Alamein. The first thing he did was criticise the COSSAC plans for being too small and put forward his own suggestions: the beachhead should be widened to include *Utah* beach in the west - making a 50 mile long zone that extended from the River Orne in the east to the Cotentin peninsula in the west - and that five divisions should be used for the assault, not three. Two airborne divisions would also cover the flanks.

His plan was for the British and Canadians to land on the easternmost beaches, and hold off the Germans, whilst the Americans landed in the west and advanced towards Cherbourg. Once that had been achieved all three armies would break out into France and thrust hard towards Germany.

Eisenhower considered the new proposals and agreed; but training the extra men and finding additional ships would take time. D-Day was put back to the beginning of June.

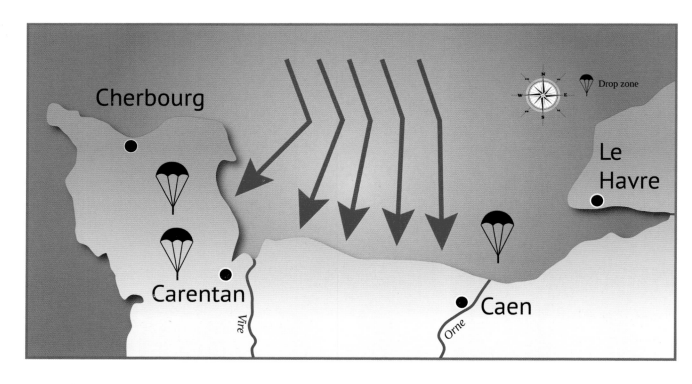

Rommel, commanding the German Army in northern France, firmly believed that 'when they come, it will be at high water'. He couldn't imagine any army choosing to land on exposed beaches at low tide where assaulting infantry would be subjected to withering fire as they crossed hundreds of yards of sand. Consequently he initiated a huge programme of installing mile after mile of metal spikes and wooden stakes, most with mines or shells attached, along all the possible beaches, designed to rip open the hulls of wooden landing craft.

Rommel's programme of beach defences was huge, and they didn't go unnoticed by Allied photo-reconnaissance. A bold decision to throw his defending army off-balance was taken: the Allies would attack when Rommel least expected it - at low-tide with the water just rising. The assault must also be at dawn, giving the invasion fleet time to cross the Channel under the cover of darkness whilst the Airborne Divisions would need a late-rising moon, so that they could make out their targets, but it must be dark enough to conceal their arrival. Only three days matched the required criteria - 5, 6 or 7 June.

The stage was now set for the largest, most complex and difficult amphibious landing ever undertaken.

Although the Americans, British and Canadians would provide the bulk of the troops and much of the naval power on D-Day, many other nations would also play their part whether on land, at sea or in the air. Polish forces, the Free French, servicemen from Czechoslovakia, the Netherlands, Belgium, Greece, Norway, Australia, South Africa, Rhodesia, and New Zealand would all be involved.

WHEN MONTY MET ROMMEL

'Before Alamein we never had a victory. After Alamein we never had a defeat'.
Winston Churchill

In October 1942, close to an insignificant, dusty desert settlement in Libya called El Alamein, the British 8th Army commanded by General Bernard Montgomery roundly defeated the hitherto victorious General Erwin Rommel and his famed *Afrika Korps*.

Some, especially the Americans, thought 'Monty' brusque, vain and even rude. Others were more generous, particularly the men under his command for whom he inspired tremendous loyalty. He was, however, a brilliant general; by the time he was appointed to command the 21st Army Group for D-Day, he had never been defeated in battle. 'Monty' placed great emphasis on overall planning, training and efficiency; in 1940 he had commanded the British 3rd Division in France, whose adept withdrawal to Dunkirk and subsequent evacuation was carried out with textbook dexterity and, compared to other units, minimal losses. Two years later, in North

Africa, he had taken over a demoralised 8th Army, rapidly re-organised it and turned it around. In a short space of time he had systematically established fresh supplies and put the army on the offensive.

Rommel, by contrast, was polite - the personification of good manners. A dashing, fast-moving tactician trained with élan in the cavalry tradition, he was well suited to the 'blitzkrieg' tank warfare that had won him fame and admiration in France in 1940. Commanding the *Afrika Korps* in the dusty, open deserts of North Africa, his quick decisions, lightning initiative and the honourable treatment of prisoners, won him the admiration of friend and foe alike. Hitler had awarded him Germany's highest honours - the Knight's Cross with Oak Leaves, Swords and Diamonds. The British, not unkindly, had awarded him a nickname 'The Desert Fox', and Winston Churchill when speaking of Rommel, had once said: 'We have a

very daring and skilful opponent against us, and, may I say across the havoc of war, a great general'.

The conflicting personalities and stratagems of the two great generals, Montgomery and Rommel, were destined to be set against each other again - in Normandy.

THE MULBERRY SOLUTION

In August 1942 five thousand Canadians, supported by a thousand Royal Marine commandos and 50 US Rangers, spearheaded a raid on the Channel port of Dieppe. It was a disaster: the intelligence was abysmal and, from well entrenched bunkers, the Germans poured down a torrent of fire on the shingle shore. Within a matter of hours, nearly 70 per cent of the force had been killed, wounded or captured.

For the crucial build-up of troops and equipment following the D-Day invasion, the Allies would need a harbour big enough to cope with the immense logistics involved. The Dieppe Raid had left the *Overlord* planners in no doubt of the perils of trying to capture a port in a head-on attack, so instead they came up with an ingenious solution: they would take their own.

Codenamed *Operation Mulberry*, two pre-fabricated artificial harbours, each bigger than the port of Dover, would be built in various discreet locations along the coast and towed across the Channel to Normandy. Here they would be quickly erected ready to receive ships laden with men, vehicles, ammunition and every other piece of equipment needed by the armies until Cherbourg could be taken.

Mulberry A would be assembled off *Omaha* beach in the American sector, Mulberry B at the British *Gold* beach at Arromanches.

The plan was simple in concept, complex in reality. As with any exposed port, each Mulberry would need breakwaters to shelter vessels from rough weather; for this task a fleet of ancient merchantmen were commandeered. Together with a group of obsolete warships they were to be stripped of their fittings, filled with concrete, sailed to Normandy under their own steam and carefully scuttled *in situ*. These sunken blockships would be supplemented by large floating concrete caissons towed across the Channel by tugs, filled with seawater and sunk. The largest of them weighed more than 6,000 tons.

Within the harbour a series of floating roadways, supported on pontoons, linked the shore to pierheads constructed from giant steel platforms, each held in place by four steel legs that could be adjusted to the rise and fall of the tide.

To create the Mulberries over a million tons of reinforced concrete and 70,000 tons of steel were used as thousands of men toiled throughout the winter and spring to complete the work. Somehow, through a mixture of brilliant engineering, clever organisation, determination and hard work, both harbours were completed in less than seven months. On D-Day plus 1, the first caissons were in place; nine days later the first vessel - an LST (Landing Ship Tank) - discharged the first vehicle, a DUKW. Mulberry was operational.

Ten days later disaster struck. The perverse Channel weather that had already forced Eisenhower to delay D-Day by a day again reared its ugly head. Throughout the night of 18 June, the pressure began to drop and, unexpectedly, the wind swung to the north-east, rising in tempo and whipping up the already choppy sea. By daybreak one of the worst storms in living memory was tearing into the Mulberries.

Terrifying waves smashed against concrete, hurricane winds screamed through steel, clawing at the metal. Pontoons, wrenched from their moorings, buckled the twisting roadways and, as sea levels rose, the caissons flooded, causing many to crack apart under the strain. Stray landing craft were tossed aside, crashing through the sides of larger vessels as the precious harbours were torn apart.

Eventually, after three days, the gale subsided but the damage was immense. The American Mulberry at *Omaha* was wrecked beyond repair; anything that could be salvaged was moved to repair the British Mulberry at Arromanches where, with superhuman effort, the artificial port was quickly back in action. By the end of the year, by which time the ports along the Channel and North Sea had been liberated, the Mulberry harbour had handled more than two million men, half a million vehicles and four million tons of supplies.

PIERS FOR USE ON BEACHES:
'They must float up and down with the tide. The anchor problem must be solved. Let me have the best solution worked out. Don't argue the matter. The difficulties will argue for themselves'.
Churchill's memo to Lord Mountbatten dated May 1942.

BRITISH MULBERRY an original drawing by Richard Taylor

Mulberry Harbour 'B' assembled off *Gold* beach at Arromanches.

SHERMAN CRAB an original drawing by Richard Taylor

With turret reversed to protect it from damage, a Sherman flail tank in action.

HOBART'S 'FUNNIES'

"...the comparatively light casualties which we sustained on all beaches, except *Omaha*, were in large measure due to the success of novel mechanical contrivances which we employed, and to the staggering moral and material effect of the mass of armour landed in the leading waves of the assault. It is doubtful if the assault forces could have firmly established themselves without the assistance of these weapons."

General Dwight D. Eisenhower's report to the Combined Chiefs of Staff on operations in Europe

Quoted by Capt. B.H.Liddell Hart-The Tanks Vol II, Cassell 1959

In March 1943 Major General Percy Cleghorn Stanley Hobart, a leading pioneer of tank warfare, was given the task of forming a new division, one that consisted entirely of specialised armoured vehicles. That unit - the 79th Armoured Division - was to play a major part in the success of the D-Day landings.

Hobart's assignment was a challenge; it required him to develop new types of armoured vehicles to help combat the multitude of defensive obstacles that littered the beaches along Hitler's much-vaunted 'Atlantic Wall'. Hobart and his team would devise tanks that swam, others to clear paths through minefields and destroy pill-boxes, lay tracks across soft sand, build bridges and climb over sea-walls - anything that would reduce the slaughter of men struggling to get ashore, as had happened at Dieppe.

There was no man better suited to the task than the inimitable Hobart and yet, if Churchill hadn't spotted a newspaper headline, the unique 79th Armoured Division might never have happened.

A veteran of the Great War, Hobart had later commanded the 1st Tank Brigade, the world's first permanent armoured unit. Then, in the desert of North Africa, he had turned the 7th Armoured Division - the 'Desert Rats' - into one of the British Army's finest units. His was the authoritative voice of modern tank warfare and his perceptive writings, especially those concerning the use of tank divisions as fast-moving, highly mobile strategic weapons, inspired the 'Blitzkrieg': General Heinz Guderian, the man who led the charge of the Panzers through France in 1940, was one of Hobart's most avid admirers.

However Hobart's brusque and outspoken manner had won him few friends in the War Office. His scathing tongue for any who didn't, or wouldn't, see the value of tanks proved too much for the entrenched, conservative minds that characterised many of the desk-bound generals in charge of the Army. In 1940, just as his country needed him, this sparkling military genius was unceremoniously forced out of the Army by what Churchill described as 'prejudices against him in certain quarters'.

As the Battle of Britain raged over southern England, and a German invasion looked possible at any moment, Hobart was 'doing his bit' as a humble lance-corporal in the Home Guard.

It was too much for the press: In August the *Sunday Pictorial* ran a story under the banner headline - 'WE HAVE WASTED BRAINS!' citing Hobart as one of the country's most wasted talents. Churchill was outraged that such a man could be sidelined, immediately writing a memo to the Chief of Imperial General Staff:

"I think very highly of this officer and I am not at all impressed by the prejudices against him in certain quarters. Such prejudices attach frequently to persons of strong personality and original view. In this case General Hobart's views have been only too tragically borne out. The neglect of the General Staff even to devise proper patterns of tanks before the war has robbed us of all the fruits of this invention. These fruits have been reaped by the enemy, with terrible consequences."

Winston Churchill - The Second World War: Vol II Their Finest Hour, The Reprint Society 1951

Eventually, thanks to Churchill's continual prodding and support, Major General Percy Hobart and his 'wasted brains' was back.

CRABS, BOBBINS AND SWIMMING TANKS

Bizarre names for strange-looking beasts maybe, but these armoured creatures saved many lives on D-Day and the war beyond.

Original drawing by Richard Taylor

THE BOBBIN

A Churchill adapted to carry a 'bobbin' or reel of heavy-duty canvas that unrolled in front of the vehicle across soft sand, or clay not substantial enough to support the weight of armoured vehicles. After the initial assault, combat engineers could lay a metal mesh track on top of it. Bobbins were to prove invaluable, especially on *Gold* where COPP parties had identified layers of soft clay running through the beach.

ARK - Armoured Ramp Carrier

A turret-less Churchill tank fitted with two ramps fore and aft of the hull for crossing small ravines.

THE CRAB

Hobart wasn't the first man to devise a rotating flail of chains mounted on a tank to clear a path through minefields; the Matilda 'Scorpion' had been invented by a South African tank officer serving in North Africa. Hobart's improved refinement - the Sherman Crab - performed valiantly on D-Day.

D7 ARMOURED BULLDOZER

An American 'Caterpillar' bulldozer fitted with armour plating and used to clear obstacles and debris from the beaches. These armoured bulldozers later proved invaluable in clearing streets full of bomb-damaged rubble.

'DD' SHERMANS

Arguably the most valuable of all Hobart's 'Funnies' on D-Day were the 'DD' - Duplex Drive - Sherman tanks that 'swam' ashore to provide artillery cover for the first assault troops. Ingeniously fitted with both tracks and propellers, 'DD' Shermans were equipped with a large flotation screen made from waterproof canvas that kept the sea water from flooding the tank. As soon as the tank hit the beach the screen was lowered and the tank performed as normal. The rough sea conditions, however, caused problems when the swimming tanks were launched too far from the shore. At *Omaha*, some of the 'DD' Shermans were launched nearly three miles off shore; many were swamped by the rough sea conditions and sank. At Utah, by contrast, the tanks were launched less than a mile from the beach and all made it safely ashore.

'BARV' Beach Armoured Recovery Vehicle

Although not strictly a 'Hobart Funny' the BARV was of the same family. Designed and operated solely by the Royal Engineers, the BARV consisted of a waterproofed Sherman tank with its turret removed and replaced with an armoured superstructure. It could operate in up to 9 foot of water and was used on D-Day to clear stranded tanks, damaged vehicles and even small landing craft away from congested beaches.

CROCODILES, SPIGOTS AND ONIONS

THE CROCODILE
Take one Churchill tank, a reinforced high-pressure nozzle instead of a machine-gun, and an armoured trailer full of fuel and the result is an armoured flame-thrower capable of propelling a 100-yard jet of flame against enemy bunkers and pill-boxes.

AVRE - Armoured Vehicle Royal Engineers
SPIGOT MORTAR
Remove the main gun from a Churchill and replace it with a thumping 40-pound mortar that fired a high-explosive shell into enemy defences such as concrete bunkers or barbed-wire entanglements.

DOUBLE ONION
An AVRE Churchill adapted to place twin high-explosive demolition charges mounted on a metal frame that could be placed against concrete walls or sea defences, and then remotely detonated from a safe distance.

PLUTO Pipe Line Under The Ocean

From within a shady cleft in the cliffs on the Isle of Wight a secret was soon unfolding after D-Day - literally. A giant coil of heavy-duty pipe slowly unravelled itself from a huge floating, 250-ton bobbin - nicknamed HMS *ConunDrum* - as it was towed away from the shore and out across the Channel towards Cherbourg at a steady 5 knots.

The local islanders knew the leafy beauty spot as Shanklin Chine; it had drawn visitors to its steep, verdant, shady paths ever since the early Victorians had discovered its appeal. To the planners of *Overlord*, however, it was the ideal place to conceal something from prying eyes because, from this idyllic spot, millions of gallons of petrol were to be pumped through a pipeline under the Channel to the fuel-thirsty armies in Normandy.

An army on the move guzzles fuel as a desert does the rain; tanks measure consumption not in miles per gallon but gallons per mile. A Sherman Firefly, racing pell-mell across country, devours petrol at the rate of about two gallons a mile - just enough to keep a Spitfire in high-octane combat for a minute or two. To fight their way across the eight hundred miles that stood between Normandy and Berlin would require a supply of fuel measured in millions of gallons. Without it the Allies would be going nowhere.

The problem facing the planners was how to get such vast quantities of what the British called petrol, and the Americans gasoline, across the Channel safely, efficiently and without the Germans guessing beforehand what was being planned. Large tankers would be vulnerable to both submarine and air attack whilst smaller vessels, on their own, could never supply the quantity required.

For the first few weeks after the invasion, five-gallon 'Jerry' cans - copied from the Germans - would have to suffice. Individually filled, then shipped and man-handled where needed, 'Jerry' cans, however, could only provide a temporary stop-gap. They weren't the answer.

The solution was ingenious: PLUTO - Pipe Line Under The Ocean - a series of flexible 3" diameter pipes, the remarkable design of which is still broadly the basis of all modern off-shore oil pipelines. Fuel, landed by tankers in the 'relative' safety of the Mersey and Bristol Channels, couldn't safely be stored in large enough quantities along the south coast without the risk of what would have to be immense silos being spotted, and probably bombed by the Germans. It would therefore have to be pumped overland to the south of England and London by pipe.

One route, code-named *Bambi*, went across country and under the Solent to the Isle of Wight. After D-Day four pipelines were to be laid on the sea-bed under the Channel to emerge at Cherbourg eighty miles away; it was the first to be used. Once the Allied armies had advanced and captured the Channel ports opposite Kent, seventeen more pipes code-named *Dumbo*, would be laid between Dungeness and Boulogne. At Dungeness construction was aided by commandeering the world's smallest public railway, the narrow-gauge Romney, Hythe and Dymchurch Railway, which also provided protection from any prying Luftwaffe eyes in the shape of a miniature armoured flak-train.

The pumping stations, necessary to push the oil from A to B, also had to be disguised. At Dungeness they were hidden as faux sea-side bungalows, on the Isle of Wight as 'Brown's ice-cream factory'. Elsewhere across the countryside, facades of genteel tea-shops and country garages camouflaged what really lay within.

Towards the final months of the war almost a million gallons of fuel per day were being pumped through PLUTO; by VE Day on 8 May 1945 the pipelines had delivered an estimated total nearing 172 million gallons.

THE DECISION TO GO

That the timeline of history was changed because of the weather was typically British. But it was the only thing that the planners couldn't control.

The week before the invasion southern England was in the grip of a heatwave; troops cursed their heavy battledress and coarse shirts as the temperatures soared. With calm seas everything was looking good until disturbing reports of falling pressure began to trickle in from ships out in the Atlantic and distant weather stations. A storm was brewing; on Monday 5 June - the planned invasion date - rough seas, torrential rain and gale force winds were predicted in the Channel.

SATURDAY 3 JUNE
SOUTHWICK HOUSE, PORTSMOUTH

Eisenhower was in a dilemma; the weather reports continued to confirm the gloomy synopsis of an approaching storm, yet looking out from Southwick House it was hard to believe. Here all was tranquil and calm. Many of the ships had been loaded by now, and some were already at sea but the Supreme Commander trusted his top weathermen. It was a tough call for him to make but, late in the evening, he ordered a temporary postponement for twenty-four hours. He confirmed his decision at dawn the following morning and D-Day was set for Tuesday 6 June when the meteorological men promised him a brief lull in the storm.

SUNDAY 4 JUNE
21.30 hours: AT SEA

All along the south coast men were cooped up below deck on wallowing ships, most were suffering badly as the intensity of the storm increased. Many were sick,

GENERAL DWIGHT D. EISENHOWER

An original drawing by Richard Taylor

and the stench of diesel and vomit was overwhelming. Officers realised that as a fighting force all keyed up and ready to go, the strength and morale of their men was being sapped. On some ships, captains and their engineers glanced with unease at falling fuel gauges. Any further delay and the entire invasion could be in jeopardy.

"By midday on 2 June we were aboard a small flat-bottomed craft holding around 150 troops – LCI 501, US Navy – which was to take us across to a still-unknown destination. Comfort aboard was almost nil. Bunks were six deep and each hold held around 50 men. The water we used for washing was seawater, and getting soap to lather from seawater is almost impossible. Killing time was our worst problem. We only went ashore once a day, for a meal.

At 9pm Monday evening we were issued with seasickness pills. That was enough; we knew by morning we should be in less peaceful waters than we were then. That evening, 501 weighed anchor. As darkness fell, we went below decks and lay on our bunks fully clothed. Outside the wind was howling even more as we turned out to sea. I dozed off before we really turned on full steam, only to be awakened by a horribly sickly feeling inside. 501 was rolling in every imaginable direction. The seasickness pills had failed if ever anything did fail. There was only one thing to do, that was to lie still; even that was dreadful and only served to make one feel worse."

Eric Broadhead of 9th Battalion, Durham Light Infantry,
The Warren Tute Collection, reproduced by kind permission of the D-Day Museum, Portsmouth.

MONDAY 5 JUNE
04.15 hours: SOUTHWICK HOUSE, PORTSMOUTH

Eisenhower was greeted by a wet and miserable dawn. Wind and rain rattled against the windows of Southwick House, but he knew that it was far worse for the men afloat. Still, the news that he received was encouraging. The promised lull in the storm was

confirmed; it would give them a window to go lasting forty-eight hours.

As the first meeting of the day got underway everyone in the room looked at Eisenhower. A rare moment of silence descended on the gathering. The destiny of Europe lay in one man's hands, he must make the call – would they go or wouldn't they?

'OK – let's go', Eisenhower quietly announced.

07.00 hrs: THE JOURNEY BEGINS

Within the next 24 hours around 130,000 Allied troops, their equipment and supplies, supported by thousands of tanks, trucks, armoured bulldozers and a mass of other vehicles, were to be transported across the Channel. They would be carried by a huge naval fleet consisting of nearly 7,000 vessels made up from almost every conceivable shape and size in an operation known as *Operation Neptune*. As Monday 5 June progressed, and well into the night, the greatest armada known to man assembled in the waters around the Isle of Wight.

At the same time the largest airborne assault ever undertaken was ready. At airfields across the southern half of England over 2,000 troop-carriers and nearly 900 gliders stood ready to embark the three Airborne Divisions who were due to land in the early hours to secure the flanks of the invasion. On almost every other runway in the country thousands of Allied aircraft prepared to provide air support.

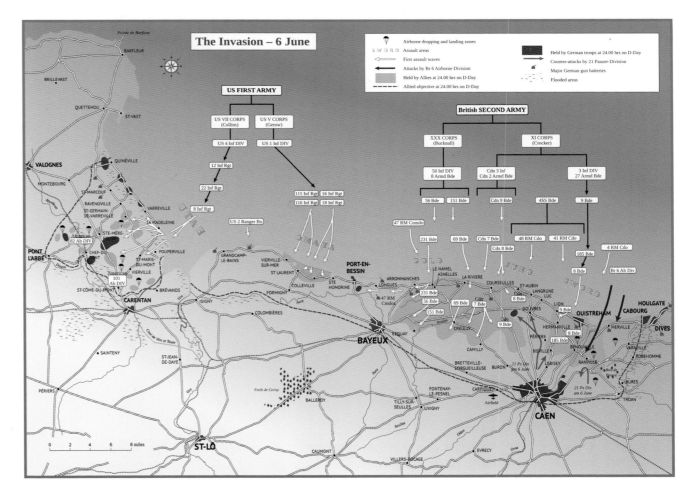

PEGASUS BRIDGE
COUP DE MAIN

OUT OF THE NIGHT – THE FIRST TO GO IN
by Robert Taylor

At 5,000 ft above the French coast the Halifax bombers release the Horsa gliders of the 'coup de main' force towards the two Orne bridges.

TUESDAY 6 JUNE
00.16 hours: THE CAEN CANAL

Silently out of the night they came. With flaps deployed, the three gliders swept down through the night skies, rapidly closing on their objective – Bénouville Bridge over the Caen Canal. On board, with tension etched deep into their blackened faces, men from the Oxfordshire & Buckinghamshire Light Infantry, part of the British 6th Airborne Division, braced themselves for what they knew was going to be a rough landing. They, and the sappers from the Royal Engineers alongside them, were led by Major John Howard, and within a few minutes they would be making history - the first fighting force to land in France on D-Day.

Their task was to capture the two Orne bridges that controlled access to the eastern flanks of *Sword* beach

where, in a few hours' time, troops of the British 3rd Division would be storming ashore. It was imperative that the German Panzers and infantry reinforcements were denied access to the vulnerable beachhead where they might throw the invasion straight back into the sea. The paratroopers must capture and hold the bridges until relieved.

Just over an hour earlier six Halifax bombers, acting as tugs, had lifted them and the other three gliders in the *coup de main* force, slowly into the air from RAF Tarrant Rushton and gently swung away from Dorset to cross the Channel on the east side of the vast invasion fleet steaming silently below them. Crossing the French coast at Cabourg, a known weak point in the German flak defences, the tow lines were cast off and the glider pilots heaved on the rudimentary controls, turning west towards

their objective and losing height as they approached the targets. Three headed for the bridge over the Orne canal – Pegasus Bridge – whilst the others aimed for the nearby Ranville Bridge over the River Orne which ran parallel to the canal.

By a feat of supreme airmanship, the three pilots at Pegasus Bridge brought their Horsa gliders down almost within touching distance of the bridge, taking the German guards by complete surprise. As the attackers tumbled half-dazed out of their battered gliders and stormed across the bridge less than a hundred yards away, a brief fire-fight ensued but, within a matter of minutes, the bridge over the canal was taken. There had been two fatal casualties, including Lieutenant Den Brotheridge who was killed leading the charge. He was the first Allied soldier to be killed in action on D-Day.

PEGASUS BRIDGE – AIRBORNE STORM by Simon Smith

At the same time, less than half a mile away, the second group had landed and captured the Ranville Bridge over the River Orne without a shot being fired. One glider, however, landed at the wrong bridge over seven miles away - resulting in a long and unexpected slog for the paratroopers through enemy lines to rejoin Allied forces.

The 6th Airborne Division, meanwhile, was being dropped just to the east of them. In the early hours the admirably named Lieutenant Colonel Pine-Coffin arrived

at the bridges with reinforcements, nearby Ranville becoming the first village in France to be liberated on D-Day. The British paratroopers were ready for the inevitable German counter-attack. It came at dawn.

Despite fierce fighting, the dogged British paratroopers held the Germans at bay until the early afternoon when Lord Lovat and the commandos of his 1st Special Service Brigade, arrived from *Sword* beach to finally push the Germans back.

'I could see it all, the river and the canal like strips of silver in the moonlight.'

Staff Sergeant Jim Wallwork DFM, pilot of the first glider to land at Pegasus Bridge.

pegasusarchive.org

FINAL DESCENT by Richard Taylor

BRITISH AIRBORNE ASSAULT

Detail from original drawing by Richard Taylor

At the same time as the two American airborne divisions were to arrive on the Cotentin, the British 6th Airborne Division, including the 1st Canadian Parachute Battalion, was dropping east of the River Orne, ready to secure the left flank. The river, and the wide canal alongside, ran due north from Caen to the sea. Beyond to the east, the River Dives ran parallel, and separating the two watercourses was a ridge on which British and Canadians would land. At the extreme northern end, where the Orne ran out into the sea, was the Merville battery. The Germans, using the same tactics that the Americans would discover in their zones, had deliberately flooded the low-lying Dives valley.

If the British could secure the ridge and blow the bridges over the Dives, then the flooded meadows would act as a defensive moat, shielding the paratroopers from any attack by the Panzers known to be nearby. Provided they could do this - and assuming that the *coup de main* force could capture and hold the bridges over the Orne - the left flank would be secure.

Commanded by the tall, imposing figure of Major-General Richard 'Windy' Gale, the British, like the Americans to the west, had suffered from a scattered drop. Although some battalions landed in their assigned zones, the bad weather and high winds had dispersed much of Gale's division. Some men found themselves landing miles away from the rendezvous points whilst others, drifting into the flood waters of the Dives, were dragged under by the weight of their equipment, and drowned.

In spite of this the British were faring better than their American counterparts. Although most battalions were at first operating well below strength, within hours stragglers were linking up with their units, although in a few cases it took men several days to find their battalions. A little over two hours after the first drop, glider-borne reinforcements arrived in strength, bringing with them jeeps, light artillery and anti-tank guns.

By dawn the 6th Airborne had achieved its objective: the bridges over the Orne had been captured and reinforced, the bridges over the Dives had been destroyed and the coastal gun battery at Merville overlooking *Sword* beach had been taken. Despite heavy fighting, the Germans were being held at bay.

SEIZING THE MERVILLE BATTERY

TUESDAY 6 JUNE

`04.00 hours: MERVILLE, 5 MILES EAST OF SWORD`

The Germans had spent two years and a lot of effort constructing the Merville battery which stared down on the small fishing port of Ouistreham at the mouth of the Orne. Allied photo-reconnaissance had studied its construction with growing concern; the battery not only covered the port and the canal to Caen, but *Sword* beach itself. If the four 150mm coastal guns it was thought to contain were brought into action, they would wreak havoc on the landings.

It would be a difficult nut to crack: the site covered more than 70 acres and was defended by prepared minefields, anti-tank ditches and barbed wire entanglements, together with a series of nearly 20 well-sited machine-gun positions. The largest of the four gun casements was known to be over 50 ft long, protected by reinforced concrete 6ft thick, covered with earth.

Any assault, least of all by lightly armed paratroopers, was going to be difficult and so an entire battalion - 9 Para, commanded by Lieutenant-Colonel Terence Otway - was assigned to the task. They would be supported by mortars, flamethrowers, mine-detectors and demolition experts, plus *a coup de main* force of gliders would land on top of the battery, much as the Germans had done at the Belgian fortress at Eben-Emael in 1940.

Unfortunately, few had fared worse from the scattered drop than 9 Para.

At 03.00 hours, two hours after they had landed, Otway had a problem: less than a quarter of his battalion and almost none of the specialised equipment had reached the rendezvous point. Against the odds he set off with around 150 men, determined to press across country as quickly and as silently as possible, praying that the reconnaissance party which had jumped earlier had reached the target before him.

Otway's tiny force now had only a couple of hours in which to succeed before the 6-inch guns of the light-cruiser HMS *Arethusa,* anchored eight nautical miles offshore, opened up in a last-ditch attempt to silence the battery.

The Germans were totally oblivious to the arrival of Otway's men, who were relieved to find that the advance party had done a superb job of cutting through the barbed wire and clearing several paths through the minefield, even though they had no detectors. Just as the *coup de main* force appeared, however, they were spotted and came under intense flak, causing the gliders to miss the target. The furore lit up the night, exposing 9 Para who immediately came under a barrage of heavy machine-gun fire. Otway gave the order to attack.

Charging forward, firing and lobbing grenades, the paratroopers, yelling wildly, sprinted towards the enemy trenches. Running a deadly gauntlet of fire, they flung themselves on the defenders in desperate, close-quarter, hand-to-hand fighting. The madcap, death-defying charge was too much for the Germans who, realising they were up against elite British paratroops, began to surrender. One by one the four casements were taken and the guns disabled - mission accomplished, but at a cost. By the end of the fire-fight only 80 of Otway's tiny, under-equipped force were in a fit state to fight. Now they must hold the position and hope for reinforcements…

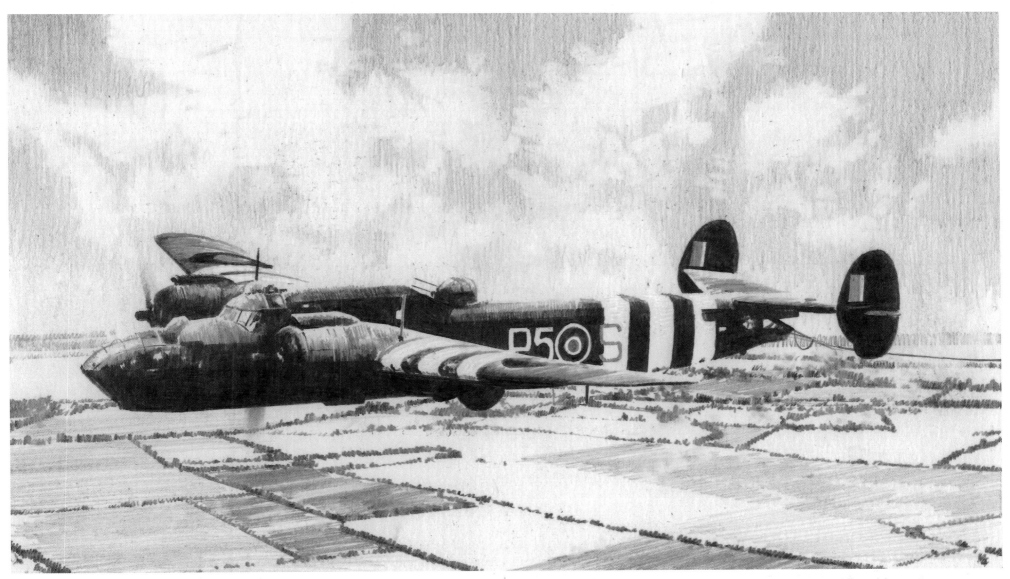

ARMSTRONG WHITWORTH ALBEMARLE
original drawing by Richard Taylor

Four squadrons of RAF Albemarle glider tugs towed Horsa
gliders for the British 6th Airborne Division on D-Day.

EVE OF DESTINY – 5 JUNE 1944 by Richard Taylor

Paratroopers of the US 101st Airborne Division prepare to board Douglas C-47s at Upottery Airfield on the eve of D-Day. Shortly after 22.00hrs they will set course for Normandy and, after crossing the French coast under heavy AA fire, drop behind Utah Beach to seize key objectives just hours before the largest seaborne invasion in history.

THE AMERICAN AIRBORNE ASSAULT

For months the two American Airborne Divisions that would fight in Normandy had prepared for this moment. Preceded by small teams of Pathfinders, the 82nd and the 101st Airborne would be amongst the first to land, and were scheduled to assault and secure the right flank of the invasion. Some, especially those in the 82nd, had already seen action but all were at the peak of readiness, an elite force ready for perhaps the most difficult jump of their lives - dropping into enemy territory at night, and under fire. The first assault of Hitler's 'Fortress Europe' was going to come from the sky and, together with the British 6th Airborne Division and the Canadian 1st Parachute Battalion, who would be landing on the left flank to the east of *Sword* beach, they formed the largest airborne force seen to date.

MISSION ALBANY and the 101st Airborne

'You have a rendezvous with destiny!' – Major General William Lee had promised his men as the 101st Airborne Division was activated at Camp Claiborne, Louisiana on 15 August 1942. And in Normandy, on the Cotentin peninsula, that rendezvous would be kept. The 101st - *The Screaming Eagles* - planned to land close behind *Utah* beach; their immediate task was to capture and secure the causeways that led down to *Utah*, cutting through swampy marshland deliberately flooded by the Germans. Without the causeways, the troops landing on the beach would have no way off. The 101st were then to secure the area closest to *Omaha* by capturing the bridges that carried the main road towards the pivotal town of

Carentan, and to seize the tidal lock on the river that ran past the town to the sea.

MISSION BOSTON and the 82nd Airborne

The 82nd Airborne Division - known as the *All American* because it was said to contain men from every state in America - would drop to the west, a little farther inland than the 101st . Theirs, too, would be a difficult jump; the area was not only low-lying and naturally boggy but, as with the marshes directly behind *Utah*, much had been flooded by the Germans. The job of the 82nd was to seize Sainte-Mère-Eglise, cut the main road and railway north to Cherbourg, and capture bridges over the River Merderet, enabling the amphibious landing on *Utah* to eventually push west and seal off the whole Cotentin peninsula.

As midnight grew closer, C-47 pilots at airfields all over the south of England first primed, then started engines. One by one, hundreds of propellers began to slowly turn before coughing into life with a gush of oily smoke. Quickly the distinctive rumble of Pratt & Whitney radials filled the air and a deep pulsating throb resonated across each base. In quick succession the fully-laden transports of the main lift lumbered across taxiways and turned on to the runway. With engines roaring at full throttle each began to move, slowly at first then, gathering speed, they were airborne. There was no going back.

The vast airborne armada was, more or less, in perfect formation as they headed south across the English coast towards the Channel Islands where they banked hard to port, heading east towards the drop-zones. It was then that the chaos began.

Flak batteries on Jersey and Guernsey had already caused problems for the pilots as they jinked to avoid the eruption of fire, but it was nothing compared to the solid bank of dense cloud they flew into as they crossed the mainland coast. With visibility down to wing-tip level, the tight formations began to break apart as many of the pilots either veered away or increased or decreased their altitude in a frantic effort to avoid a mid-air collision. Approaching the drop-zones the cloud thinned but the flak dramatically increased. Several planes were hit and fell blazing to the ground. If the turbulence through the cloud had been unsettling, the concussion from exploding cannon shells was terrifying as the aircraft, and their occupants, were tossed and pitched through the mêlée of flame and smoke.

Then it was time to jump. For a few unlucky souls whose C-47s had flown too low, their parachutes never had time to open, others landed in flooded fields and were drowned, dragged under by the weight of their equipment. Many were machine-gunned as they drifted slowly down but the majority made it safely to earth. They soon found out that they had been scattered far and wide and that it was going to be a long and difficult night.

MONDAY 5 JUNE
22.15 hours: UPOTTERY AIRFIELD

Early in the evening of 5 June Eisenhower had been driven 50 miles north from his headquarters at Southwick House near Portsmouth to Newbury. He arrived unexpectedly at RAF Greenham Common to wish the paratroopers of the 502nd Parachute Infantry Regiment, 101st Airborne good luck as they prepared their kit, ready to board the waiting lines of C-47s from the 438th Troop Carrier Group. These youngsters would be some of the first into action.

It was a great morale boost as he walked amongst them, chatting casually to NCOs and enlisted men alike, calming nerves. Visibly moved, he waited patiently beside the runway until they were all airborne before returning to Portsmouth.

At a dozen airfields stretching from Devon in the west to Lincolnshire in the east, just over 13,000 men from the 82nd and 101st were also getting ready. Whilst Eisenhower was busy at Greenham Common, a hundred miles away in Devon at Upottery, C-47s of the 439th Troop Carrier Group were preparing to embark another unit of the 101st - the 506th Parachute Infantry Regiment, and the men of *Easy* Company, 2nd Battalion.

LONG HARD ROAD by Robert Taylor

The men of *Easy Company*, 2nd Battalion, 506th Parachute Infantry Regiment, check their equipment one last time before boarding the C-47s that will carry them from Upottery in Devon to Normandy. This would be the start of a long, often bloody yet heroic trail that would take them from Normandy, through the horrors of the Battle of the Bulge to the capture of Hitler's mountain retreat, the 'Eagle's Nest' at Berchtesgaden. An epic story later made famous in the award-winning TV series *Band of Brothers*.

TUESDAY 6 JUNE
01.40 hours: COTENTIN PENINSULA

Within most Airborne Divisions there existed individual units that stood out from the rest, and one or two within the 101st were no different. Perhaps the most notorious of them all was a small bunch of raw, tough, ruthless young men, mostly from the Dustbowl, with scant regard for authority - men who had withstood the worst that the Depression could throw at them. Hard-drinking and savage fighters - and that was only in training – they were never ones to salute an officer, clean their uniforms and, in the weeks before D-Day, seldom took a bath. Officially they were the First Section of the Demolition Platoon, Regimental HQ Company, 506th Parachute Infantry Regiment. Unofficially they were the 'Filthy Thirteen'.

And if the reputation of this unique bunch of renegades within the ranks of the 'Screaming Eagles' was formidable, for the Germans it would become one of terror because, for the 'Filthy Thirteen', anything not directly concerned with killing the enemy was irrelevant. Theirs was a story so bizarre that it became the inspiration for the Hollywood blockbuster *The Dirty Dozen'*.

D-DAY DROP - STICK 21 by Robert Taylor

Robert Taylor's dramatic drawing depicts the moment that this elite platoon jump from their C-47 into the battle below. As deadly flak pummels the formation the young pilot from the 96th TCS, 440th TCG at the control of C-47 *6Z*, wrestles with the controls, trying to keep his aircraft level and steady amidst the turbulence.

D-DAY - THE AIRBORNE ASSAULT by Robert Taylor

03.45 hours: THE FOLLOW UP

Following hard on the heels of the parachute forces, by now scattered but fighting hard, came the first of the glider reinforcements. Using CG-4A WACO gliders, the rough terrain caused problems but they had brought with them much-needed equipment, including jeeps and anti-tank guns.

Later, in the evening of D-Day, in a scene portrayed by Robert Taylor's famous painting - *D-Day - The Airborne Assault* - seen above, a further glider lift of reinforcements arrived, this time covered by a heavy screen of fighters. Seen crossing the Normandy beaches just after 21.00 hrs on D-Day are C-47s of the 438th

Troop Carrier Group towing CG-4A WACO gliders from Greenham Common carrying additional elements of the 82nd Airborne. Closely escorted by P-51Bs of the 354th Fighter Group, the pilots can't fail to be impressed by the scene on the ground as landing craft swarm ashore, putting yet more men and equipment on the beaches.

LIBERATION

TUESDAY 6 JUNE
`04.30 hours:` SAINTE MÈRE-EGLISE

For nearly four years the swastika had flown belligerently over the small town of Sainte Mère-Église, positioned on the main road north to Cherbourg five miles inland from the sandy dunes of *Utah* beach.

Those four years had passed in relative peace until, shortly after midnight on the night of 5/6 June 1944, a fire broke out in a house on the town square. It was probably caused by a pathfinder's flare. As the townsfolk battled to staunch the blaze, tongues of flame lit up the night sky. Almost immediately the white silk of blossoming parachutes were spotted in the orange glow. A startled cry went up amongst the local German garrison of anti-aircraft gunners - Fallschirmjägers!

Paratroopers from the 505th Parachute Infantry Regiment, 82nd Airborne Division were landing. D-Day had arrived at Sainte Mère-Église.

For those of the 505th dropping into the town, the view beneath them was not a pretty one. Illuminated by the fire, the Germans had them clearly in their sights and the paratroopers could only watch in horror as machine-gun and tracer fire arced up towards them. Many were riddled with bullets before they had even touched the soil of France. Those who did survive the landing were then either killed or captured. One of them, John Steele, landed on the church, his chute caught on the steeple. He was captured but later escaped. For the 505th it was a gruesome beginning.

A mile or so away the scene was better: Lieutenant-Colonel Ed Kruse - commander of the 505th PIR - had quickly gathered enough of his men together and dashed towards the town, overwhelming the German defenders after a brief exchange of fire. By 04.30 hours the 505th raised another flag over the town – the Stars and Stripes. Sainte Mère Église had become the first town in Normandy to be liberated by the Americans.

$\longrightarrow$

LIBERATION - SAINTE MÈRE ÉGLISE
by Richard Taylor

Sherman tanks, recently landed on nearby *Utah* beach with the US VII Corps, pass through Sainte Mère Église shortly after the town had been liberated by the 82nd Airborne Division. The church tower, which had witnessed much of the fighting, still supports the tattered parachute of Private John Steele.

D-DAY NORMANDY LANDINGS by Robert Taylor

Brigadier Sir Alex Stanier Bt DSO MC, who commanded the 231st Brigade (50th Northumbrian Division) on the west sector of
Gold beach 6 June 1944, said of this famous painting: "I have never seen a better or more accurate depiction of the landings.
Robert Taylor did his research well, down to the exact state of the sea and weather".

THE AMPHIBIOUS LANDINGS

6 JUNE 1944

Were the invasion to happen in Normandy, few at German Army headquarters in Paris - OB West (Oberbefehlshaber West) - believed it would come today, including the Commander-in-Chief, Generalfeldmarschall Gerd von Rundstedt.

For the week ahead the Luftwaffe meteorologists had, like their Allied counterparts, predicted rough seas in the Channel, whipped up by strong winds. The Germans, however, lacking the more accurate details from the deep Atlantic available to the Allies, had failed to spot the information that had been given to Eisenhower the day before yesterday: a window of 48 hours' 'relative' calm passing through the

Channel. And that window began this morning…

Believing the invasion highly unlikely this week, many senior German officers had been ordered to attend 'war-games' in Rennes, ironically in preparation for a possible airborne assault. Feldmarschall Rommel, who commanded Army Group B, the land forces in northern France, had taken the opportunity to travel to Germany to visit his wife, before attending a meeting with Hitler at which he was going to press the Führer for more, and better, troops.

The rumours started just after midnight. British glider-borne forces had seized two bridges over the

Orne, just north of Caen and further to the west; flak batteries were reporting seeing hundreds of aircraft overhead. Then more persistent reports began to come in of paratroopers landing in their thousands; there was fighting in a wide area near Sainte Mère-Église, and in several places to the east of the River Orne. Some large ships had apparently been spotted at sea and talk of telephone lines being cut by saboteurs filtered through. Was this all part of a raid, a diversionary attack? Or was it the prelude to something bigger and much more dangerous - the invasion itself?

FROM SHIP TO SHORE

After the horrifying carnage on the shingle shores of Dieppe in 1942, the lesson had been learnt; it would be suicide for any invading army to attempt a landing and the capture of a large Channel port from the sea. For D-Day to succeed, therefore, the assault would have to be made on wide open beaches - and that meant building landing craft, thousands of them.

Without landing craft it would be impossible to land the vast numbers of men, equipment and the matériel needed to establish the bridgehead so pivotal to the entire *Overlord* plan. And there would have to be many different types of landing craft capable of carrying out a myriad of tasks: small LCAs to land the first assault teams on the beach, large ocean-going vessels to carry the heavy tanks, artillery, ammunition and equipment. There would have to be vessels to provide close fire-support on the beaches, floating anti-aircraft batteries in case of air attack, landing craft adapted to launch a terrifying barrage of rockets against enemy positions, and even floating barges equipped as kitchens to feed the crews who didn't have their own galleys.

For more than a year shipyards across the length of both Britain and North America had been working flat-out to construct the large, ocean-going landing ships. Slipways sparkled with welders' flashes and docks resonated to the deep clanging of heavy metal being worked. Smaller yards that, before the war, had once crafted wood into fishing boats, wherries or even beautiful yachts now turned their wood-working skills into making parts to build the small wooden landing craft being assembled in factories that in peace-time had built tables and chairs. These ungainly, flat-bottomed little craft, needed to carry the infantry on to the beaches, were poor sailors that heaved, pitched and rolled in choppy seas so that many of those landing on D-Day were suffering from sea-sickness.

The number of vessels directly involved in *Operation Neptune* was mind-boggling: apart from 1,213 naval warships, 4,126 landing ships and landing craft, 736 ancillary craft and 864 merchant vessels were involved in the landings whilst some 195,700 personnel - 112,824 British, 52,889 American and 4,988 from other Allied countries - were assigned to the operation.

LCA - Landing Craft Assault

With a crew of four, LCAs could carry a platoon of 36 troops (or an equivalent amount of supplies) directly on to the beach. They were just over 40ft long and 10ft wide, and usually armed with two .303 machine-guns and a Bren light machine-gun.

LCVP - Landing Craft Vehicle/ Personnel

Also known as the *Higgins Boat* after the designer whose firm first built them, LCVPs had the capacity to carry 36 troops, or a jeep and 12 men, or supplies. With a crew of four they were slightly shorter than an LCA, but wider.

LCI(L) - Landing Craft Infantry (Large)

Larger sea-going landing craft capable of carrying over 200 infantry who landed on the beach via two ramp walkways either side of the bow. Typically armed with three 2-pound and four 20mm Oerkilon cannons, LCIs were approximately 158 ft long and 23 ft wide.

LCT - Landing Craft Tank

Transporting up to six medium tanks depending on their size, or trucks, or 136 tons of cargo, they were crewed by a single officer and 12 crew. LCTs were widely used on D-day.

LSI - Landing Ship Infantry

These were larger troopships, typically converted from pre-war cross-channel ferries and small passenger liners. LSIs were used to transport large quantities of troops from the embarkation ports to a safe distance offshore from where they would be transferred into LCAs hung on davits each side. The size of each ship was identified either as an **LSI(S)** Small or an **LSI(L)** - Large.

OPERATION OVERLORD by Richard Taylor

LST - Landing Ship Tank in the USN or **TLS - Tank Landing Ship** in the Royal Navy these purpose-built ocean-going ships, usually about 400 ft long, were capable of carrying around 20 tanks or heavy trucks, plus 200 men. Landing craft were also adapted for other specialist tasks, such as:

LCA(H) - Landing Craft Assault (Hedgehog) were fitted with four rows of 6 spigot high-explosive mortars - adapted from ship-borne anti-submarine weapons known in the Navy as 'Hedgehogs'. These were used to suppress beach defences.

LCG(L) - Landing Craft Gun (Large) were modified LCTs typically fitted with artillery to give a close off-shore barrage. They were usually equipped with eight 20mm Oerlikon cannons and a pair of 25-pounder Howitzer field guns .

LCT(F) - Landing Craft Tank (Flak) crewed by 60 Royal Marines LCT(F)s provided anti-aircraft cover with quadruple Vickers 'pom-pom' anti-aircraft guns and eight 20mm Oerlikon cannon.

LCT(R) - Landing Craft Tank (Rocket) were devastating weapons capable of firing a thousand rockets at a time, each with a 65-pound warhead, the equivalent firepower of over 60-cruisers.

LCS - Landing Craft Support typically armed with twin .5 machine-guns plus a 4-inch smoke mortar. Larger versions - **LCS(L)** - had additional anti-tank guns and an armoured turret containing a 25-pound field gun mounted on the fore-deck.

LCM - Landing Craft Mechanised designed to ferry vehicles ashore and not forgetting the **LBK - Landing Barge Kitchens** that provided hot and cold meals to the crews of the small landing craft. LBKs were moored off all five beaches on D-Day.

DUKW

Although not strictly landing craft, DUKWs played a very important role on and after D-Day transporting men and supplies. These six-wheel drive amphibious trucks were based on the US Army's 2-ton truck built by General Motors. The letters DUKW are not an acronym but are letters making up a General Motors assembly code:

    D – denoted a vehicle designed in 1942

    U – denoted a 'Utility' vehicle

    K – Power-driven front wheels

    W – Power-driven twin rear axles.

UTAH DAWN by Anthony Saunders

Just before H-Hour on 6 June 1944, the growing light reveals B-26 Marauders of the 553rd Bomb Squadron, 386th Bomb Group, escorted by B-51Bs, heading over *Utah* beach to attack the coastal gun batteries. In the foreground is B-26 'Dinah Might', flown by Major David H. Dewhurst Jr. Below them, they and the other Marauder crews witness the vast amphibious assault force heading steadily towards the Normandy shore.

UTAH DAWN

TUESDAY 6 JUNE

05.05 hours: UTAH BEACH

D-Day Objective: To gain a secure beachhead from which to capture the Cotentin Peninsula and then the port of Cherbourg.

At *Utah* the approaching light of dawn revealed the first distant glimpse of something no German soldier had seen before. Peering seaward from their concrete casements, the watchers stood momentarily stunned by what lay before their eyes - the grey ghost of a vast invasion fleet closing with the shore. It was 05.05 hours and immediately the first German batteries opened fire.

In the landing craft wallowing awkwardly in the choppy water offshore, the assault parties of the US 4th Infantry Division ducked involuntarily as the first shells screamed high overhead towards the dark warships silhouetted on the horizon. For most of them these were the first shots they had heard fired in anger.

The big naval guns of the fleet instantly replied and then, above the noise of the big-gun duel came the drone of heavy aero engines; a force of over 250 B-26 Marauder medium bombers swept overhead to unleash their deadly cargos, effectively destroying many of the gun pits and strong-points on the gently sloping foreshore.

At 06.30 hours the ramps of the first landing craft slammed down and the 8th Infantry Regiment hit the beach, followed by the first of the Sherman 'DD' swimming tanks emerging from the surf. Everyone soon realised that strong rip currents had caused a navigational error; the Americans had landed a mile or so south of their intended beach. It turned out, however, to be a blessing in disguise - the beach on which they landed was only lightly defended.

With the tide rising steadily, more and more men poured ashore, including specialist demolition squads and engineers with armoured bulldozers who were quickly in action clearing the stakes, mines and other beach obstacles. Within three hours routes off the beach had been secured, allowing more battalions to land and together press on to link up with the 101st Airborne still fighting fiercely inland.

By midnight 23,250 troops had been landed on *Utah* and, in stark contrast to what was happening on nearby *Omaha*, there were fewer than 200 casualties.

ADVANCE FROM UTAH by Simon Smith

Shortly after destroying the Brécourt Manor battery the men of Easy Company await orders from Dick Winters, their new commanding officer. The young lieutenant, whose leadership and tactical skills will, over the next few months, become legendary, carefully considers their next objective – the advance towards Carentan.

BRÉCOURT MANOR

TUESDAY 6 JUNE
`08.30 hours:` THREE MILES SOUTH-WEST OF UTAH BEACH

It had been a rough ride in for the men of *Easy* Company dropping into the night inland from *Utah* beach. Their C-47s had run into turbulent clouds as they crossed the French coast, followed by heavy German flak. Then their commanding officer had been killed and when they'd finally hit the silk they, like much of the 101st Airborne, had been dropped off target: men, weapons and supplies scattered over miles. In a few hours' time, however, the leading units of the largest amphibious force in history would be hitting the beaches. The area behind *Utah* must be secured.

It had taken till dawn for First Lieutenant Dick Winters to gather enough individual soldiers together and now his small force of less than a dozen men had been ordered to take a battery of four German 105mm Howitzers, located just inland at Brécourt Manor. The enemy guns were zeroed in, blocking a route off the beach; if the guns couldn't be eliminated then the landing was in trouble.

The German defenders were well prepared with machine-gun pits and entrenched mortar nests hidden by dense hedgerows and linked by a series of well concealed trenches. And if that wasn't enough, Winters guessed rightly that he was probably heavily outnumbered.

Using his little group's one mortar and two light machine-guns to suppress the enemy fire, Winters rapidly put in a lightning flanking attack, the speed of which stunned the enemy into submission. After a brief but intense fire-fight the men of *Easy* Company seized and destroyed all four of the big Howitzers but a row of machine-guns along a hedgerow close to the manor house held out until a couple of Sherman tanks rumbled up from the beach. Letting loose a barrage of heavy-calibre cannon fire, the tanks ripped the hedgerow apart.

Winters and his little band now awaited orders for their next objective - CARENTAN.

SAINTE MARIE-DU-MONT

The village of Ste Marie-du-Mont, with its distinctive church and imposing tower, lies in open country a few miles inland from *Utah* beach. Within the village dozens of German artillerymen, who manned the nearby strong-points and the bunkers on the beach, were quartered. Surrounded by the countryside and far from the East Front it had, until now, been a good billet. Now it was slap in the middle of one of the 101st Airborne's drop-zones.

As with almost every other drop, the American paratroopers had been scattered over a wide area, but gradually mixed units formed up and were soon attacking the strong-points and the village. The 101st stormed through the streets, house by house, and in the face of such ferocity the Germans began to surrender. White flags appeared from doorways and windows whilst others slipped away as fast as they could. It wasn't long before tanks and infantry were swarming through the village square towards the main road towards Carentan.

THE ROAD FROM UTAH - Ste Marie-du-Mont by Simon Smith

Paratroopers of the 101st Airborne lead American armoured units through the recently liberated village of Sainte Marie-du-Mont just inland from *Utah* beach. Overhead is the welcoming site of a pair of P-51 Mustangs covering the beach-head.

ANGOVILLE-AU-PLAIN

IN HONOUR AND IN RECOGNITION OF

ROBERT E. WRIGHT

KENNETH J. MOORE

MEDICS 2nd Bn 501 PIR

101st AIRBORNE DIVISION

FOR HUMANE AND LIFE-SAVING CARE RENDERED TO 80

COMBATANTS AND A CHILD IN THIS CHURCH IN JUNE 1944

TUESDAY 6 JUNE
SIX MILES SOUTH-WEST OF UTAH BEACH

Those are the simple words, carved into the stone memorial outside a little church in Normandy, that recall the heroic actions of two medics who found themselves setting up a field dressing-station here in the early hours of D-Day.

The two men had been amongst the last elements of the 101st to drop in the early hours of D-Day, their landing zone just south of Sainte Marie-du-Mont. By the time their C-47s had arrived the Germans were wide awake and ready for the paratroopers landing in their midst. If the unit thought the approach had been rough, it was nothing compared to the reception waiting for them on the ground.

Moore and Wright soon found themselves in the middle of a bitter, confused and savage fire-fight centred on the tiny hamlet of Angoville-au-Plain. Setting up residence in the ancient 12th century village church, the two medics started treating the first of the wounded as the battle swirled around the gravestones outside. Irrespective of the uniform they wore, the wounded of both sides were treated just the same.

Over the next couple of days, possession of the little hamlet changed hands several times as the fight ebbed and flowed around the church. As mortars fell, shaking plaster from the time-worn walls on to the flagstones below, the statues of 3rd century Saints Comas and Damian - twin brothers who are the patron saints of surgeons and physicians, to whom the church was dedicated, looked down on the two Airborne medics below.

And still the wounded came; the plain wooden pews, now stained with blood, listening silently to soldiers' simple prayers. Two little French girls, badly injured in the fighting outside, were brought in, too, joining the mass of men.

Throughout the raging battle there was, however, one simple rule. No guns were to be brought inside the church. The first time two German paratroopers had burst through the big oak doors, machine-guns raised to their hips, the US medics looked them straight in the eye and nodded down at a wounded German lying at their feet. The two enemy paratroopers understood, both saluted and immediately withdrew.

By the time the fighting finally subsided, all but three of the 80 wounded had survived. Sadly one of the little girls was amongst the three who didn't.

'WE TREATED THEM ALL THE SAME' by Simon Smith

Regardless of their uniform, every wounded soldier brought to the field dressing station within the tiny church at Angoville-au-Plain was treated equally by two heroic US Medics from the 101st Airborne.

POINTE DU HOC

TUESDAY 6 JUNE

07.10 hours: FOUR MILES WEST OF OMAHA

The Germans had done their work well: the Allies considered the Pointe du Hoc as probably the most dangerous battery on the entire Normandy coast. Only in the Pas de Calais were the fortifications thought to be stronger.

On this high rocky promontory jutting out into the sea four miles to the west of *Omaha* beach, it was believed that up to six 155mm field guns – ironically captured from the French in 1940 - threatened not only both American beaches but, with a range of over twelve miles, the ships of the bombarding fleet.

Protected to seaward by near-vertical cliffs that towered over the merest hint of beach below, and on the land side by an intricate web of defences screened by minefields and secured by Germany infantry, the artillery garrison in their reinforced bunkers felt secure. Secure, that is, until American and British bombers had appeared in force a couple of months earlier, their bombs rendering the ground into a morass of craters. But despite the scale of the bombing the guns, in their deeply embedded concrete casements, remained unscathed.

Reports from the local French Resistance, however, indicated that the bombing raids had provoked the Germans into removing the guns to a safe distance a mile or so inland. But had they? Was it possible that some or all of them remained or, if some had been removed, had they now been returned and were once again ready to hurl shells onto the invading fleet?

No one was quite sure but whatever the answer, the Pointe du Hoc was, guns or no guns, the perfect position from which the Germans could observe and bring down fire on the beaches in either direction..

The task of attacking this seemingly impregnable strongpoint was not for the faint-hearted, and was given to three companies of the US 2nd Ranger Battalion, led by Lieutenant Colonel James Rudder. For months the Rangers, volunteers to a man, had undergone the gruelling commando course at the British Commando School in Scotland. Then had come the specialised assault training where, using rocket-propelled grapnels, ropes and extending ladders – courtesy of London Fire Brigade - mounted on amphibious DUKWs, they prepared specifically for the assault on the Pointe du Hoc. Although it would be their first combat operation, by the time they embarked at Weymouth, the Rangers were a finely-honed unit ready for battle.

At 05.50 hours on the morning of 6 June the battleship *USS Texas* opened fire on the Pointe du Hoc. It was an awe-inspiring broadside, all ten of her massive 14" main guns firing in a single, simultaneous salvo. It was the first of many. Over the next 25 minutes the valiant old battleship, a veteran of World War 1, poured salvo after salvo onto the target. Huge chunks of concrete and rock erupted skywards, boulders the size of trucks crashing down into the broiling sea below.

Meanwhile, the Rangers approaching the Pointe du Hoc were being soaked to the skin by rain and drenching spray. But a soaking was the least of their problems because, as so often in war, things were starting to go wrong.

Already three of their landing craft had either capsized or been swamped by the heavy swell, and one of the DUKWs hit by enemy fire. Now, affected by unusually strong currents, the remainder found themselves veering too far east. The next 35 minutes were spent fighting wind and tide as they battled to get back to their right beach. It cost them valuable time, for which they paid dearly; the delay allowing the Germans to prepare a hostile welcome. When the Rangers finally hit the beach they were greeted by a shower of grenades hurled from the cliff top above. Luckily at that moment a well-aimed and well-timed broadside from an American destroyer forced the Germans back.

The pebble beach they had landed on was pocket-sized, made smaller by the fast-rising tide. The tumbled scree of boulders, remnants of the *Texas'* broadsides, straddled the foreshore meaning the DUKWs couldn't get close enough to the cliff face for the ladders to reach.

Things went from bad to worse when many of the rocket-propelled grapnels failed to reach the top; the ropes, saturated with water, were too heavy. The Rangers were taking casualties; using the few ropes that had taken hold, they had to get up and off the beach fast.

It was now, as the adrenaline kicked in, that all those punishing hours of training paid off. Climbing quickly, hand over hand, the first were atop the cliff within minutes and, firing like demons, forced the Germans to retreat. All they had to do now was spike the guns - guns that had remained ominously silent. The reason for that silence was soon apparent. The rumours had been right: the guns had been removed - but to where?

Colonel Rudder quickly sent out patrols in search of their quarry and ninety minutes later they found them, hidden in an orchard and trained directly on *Utah* beach, ready to fire. To the Rangers' astonishment the guns were unguarded, and a handful of thermite grenades soon put them out of action. Now they had to consolidate their position, repel any counter-attacks, and wait for reinforcements. It turned out to be a long and painful wait because, unknown to the colonel and his men, the situation on *Omaha* beach was not going well.

USS TEXAS original pencil drawing by Richard Taylor

THE HELL CALLED OMAHA

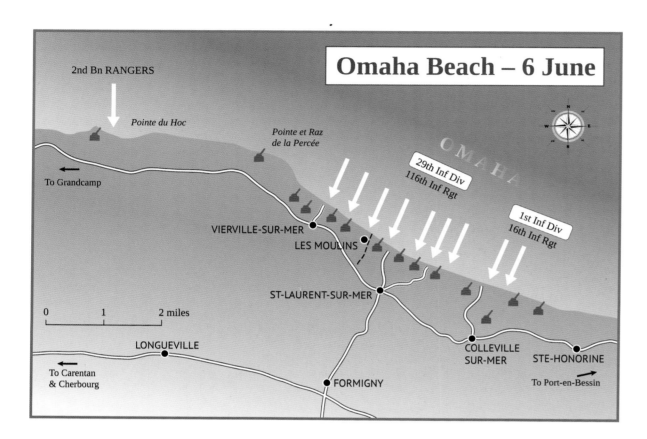

Omaha Beach – 6 June

2nd Bn RANGERS

Pointe du Hoc

Pointe et Raz de la Percée

29th Inf Div 116th Inf Rgt

1st Inf Div 16th Inf Rgt

OMAHA

To Grandcamp

VIERVILLE-SUR-MER

LES MOULINS

ST-LAURENT-SUR-MER

0   1   2 miles

LONGUEVILLE

COLLEVILLE SUR-MER

STE-HONORINE

To Carentan & Cherbourg

FORMIGNY

To Port-en-Bessin

D-Day Objectives: To establish a link between the American troops at *Utah* beach and the two US Airborne Divisions, and the British and Canadian beaches to the east.

Everyone knew *Omaha* was going to be a brute, they had known it from the day that *Overlord* had been agreed. Here, however, on a crescent-shaped beach four miles wide, was the only place on the coast linking isolated *Utah* in the west to *Gold* to the east where a landing could possibly take place.

The problem was the terrain; it was a defender's dream. Overlooking the beach from behind were ridges of high, undulating bluffs that merged into formidable 100-foot high cliffs on either flank. The only way inland

lay up through five eroded gullies that ran haphazardly up through the lumpy ground. At high tide the beach was reduced to a few yards of shingle; at low tide there were four hundred yards of wet sloping sand. There was no cover and troops would not only be subjected to full frontal fire coming from strong-points hidden in the bluffs, but they would be raked by enfilading artillery and machine-gun fire from the cliffs on the flanks. The Germans had had all the time in the world to prepare their killing zones. It would be a tough nut to crack.

And, unknown to the Allies, the German troops stationed on *Omaha* were in greater numbers than intelligence had suggested. As with many well-thought-out plans, in the fog of war this, combined with sheer bad luck, led to the nightmare known as '*Bloody Omaha*'.

TUESDAY 6 JUNE
06.35 hours: OMAHA BEACH

All through the night the Allied forces had endured an uncomfortable, rough crossing. Many, already queasy with nerves, were sea-sick and matters didn't improve when, shortly after 04.00 hours, the troops who would lead the assault wave transferred into their small landing craft miles off-shore.

Buffeted by the rough sea, several craft were swamped and sank whilst on the rest men, soused by spray and rain, braced themselves and huddled low amidst the stench of vomit.

The tiny craft pitched and lurched slowly towards the beach, now almost obscured from view by mist and smoke from the preceding air raid. The men had raised a ragged cheer as the bombs had fallen but what they didn't know was that the airmen, fearing to hit the landing craft, had delayed releasing their loads by a few precious seconds. Most bombs had exploded harmlessly far inland.

It was now 06.35 hours; with a sickening crunch the first landing craft hit the beach and the ramps crashed down. With gritted teeth the first wave charged forward; only to be met by a blizzard of fire. In places men stepped into neck-high water and, where seconds earlier they had been a fighting unit, now they were desperate individuals seeking only to survive. Yard by yard a bloody trail was being left across the sand as survivors grimly fought their way up the killing-ground that was called a beach. In waters now stained by blood the dead, caressed by the incoming tide, collected in heaps amongst the breaking surf. Over the thump of exploding mortars and unending staccato of machine-gun fire could be heard the screams and the pleading cries of the wounded, some unable to escape the fast-rising tide.

The infantry had expected there to be many more tanks alongside them, but only five of the swimming Shermans had made it, the rest had foundered in the rough sea. Those that did make it gave what support they could. Apart from the swimming tanks and a few

ASSAULT ON OMAHA BEACH by Simon Smith

LIGHTNINGS OVER THE NORMANDY BEACHES an original pencil drawing by Richard Taylor

armoured bulldozers, the Americans didn't use the heavily armoured, beach-clearing equipment attached to the British divisions. With no paths cleared, when the second wave arrived an hour after the first, they just added to the chaos and confusion and, as the tide advanced higher and higher the packed shoreline got ever narrower. At one point the situation was so critical that Lieutenant General Omar Bradley, commanding the US 1st Army, came within an ace of calling the *Omaha* landing off.

Assisted by fire from those tanks that had got ashore, from destroyers off-shore and helped by the impetus of newly-landed Rangers, the flanking cliffs were slowly cleared. Down on the beach the determination and bravery of a few individuals and small groups of men was beginning to have an effect on the Germans as their ammunition ran low. One by one the strong-points were gradually taken out, barbed wire entanglements demolished and paths cleared through the mines. But it was grim work and the casualties rose yet, bit by bit, scattered groups slowly advanced. By midday, although still under heavy fire, units had broken through far enough to establish a secure exit off the beach. By the middle of the afternoon the first tanks were heading inland.

It had been a terrible day's fighting, especially for the first assault teams but, by midnight, 34,250 troops had been landed - more than on any other beach - and a small bridgehead formed. Amid the savage fighting three men would be awarded the Congressional Medal of Honor - America's highest award for valour. But success had come at a price. Unlike the almost text-book landings at *Utah*, where less than two hundred men had been casualties, *Omaha* had claimed ten times that number.

'Every man who set foot on Omaha beach that day was a hero.'

General Omar Bradley

BRITISH GOLD

"The sea was rough. This in itself complicated the landing. Around 7am we were ordered to dress with all kit. We were below decks, wondering what was going on. Heavy naval gunfire could be heard. 501 had landing ramps which dropped down from her side into the sea, or the beach where it was possible for her to nose far enough in. It was when these ramps dropped we knew the voyage was over. We scrambled on deck. The kit we had was terrific – waterproof jackets that came up to one's chest from one's feet, these I tore as I struggled on deck. Ahead only a matter of yards away was the French coast, but it was too far away to keep dry. Naval personnel were shouting 'Get ashore', ships were everywhere like a traffic jam. Down the ramps we went, but this only led into the ship in front, across its decks, then came 10 horrible yards between ship and shore with water in between. Over the ship's side, still dizzy from seasickness, and into water 4 ft deep. Each one of us let out a gasp as the water swirled around, and we struggled for shore. It was the hardest ten yards I ever did, but we all got ashore. It became apparent that the enemy had been taken by surprise, at least on our particular section of the attack. After five minutes re-grouping as a battalion, I saw a real life German soldier for the first time. He was being brought in as a prisoner by the lads who beat us ashore."

Eric Broadhead, 9th Battalion, Durham Light Infantry, landed on *Gold* beach from the US Landing Craft Infantry (LCI) 501.

Warren Tute Collection, D-Day Museum Portsmouth

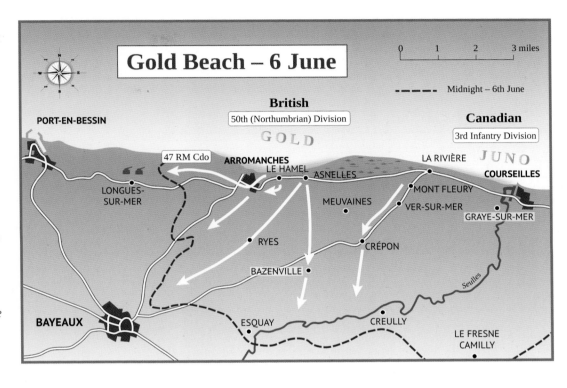

D-Day Objectives: To capture Bayeux and the main RN13 towards Caen, and to link up with the Americans on *Omaha*.

With the tide flowing eastward up the Channel, low-water on the British *Gold* beach would be an hour later than at *Utah* and *Omaha*. The assault would be carried out by the British 50th (Northumbrian) Division, supported by the 8th Armoured Brigade.

TUESDAY 6 JUNE
07.25 hours: GOLD BEACH

As with the two beaches in the American sector, a fierce naval bombardment preceded the landings as salvos of 6" inch shells from the cruisers screamed down on the German positions. The fleet, anchored six miles off *Gold*, included the light cruiser HMS *Ajax* that had gained fame with the sinking of the German pocket-battleship *Admiral Graf Spee* at the Battle of the River Plate in 1939.

For the Germans hunkered down in their casements the barrage was terrifying, the tumultuous detonations increasing as Allied bombers joined in with the bombardment. The entire stretch of coast fronted by the seaside villages of Le Hamel and La Rivière, together with nearby coastal gun batteries, rocked with shock and concussion.

At *Gold* the water was just as rough, the wind equally blustery as the Americans had encountered at *Omaha*. For the soaked infantry, huddled and crouched close together in the lurching LCAs heading for the shore, it was the worst of journeys. The coxswains struggling to hold their headings as the strong currents plucked at

MARINES ON GOLD by Simon Smith

Under heavy fire, and with four of their landing craft sunk on the approach, 47 Royal Marines Commando land on *Gold* beach, tasked with the capture of Port-en-Bessin. Major General Julian Thompson described their exploits as 'one of the finest feats of arms of any unit, Royal Marines, Army, Navy or Air Force of any nation in the Second World War'.

their fragile craft. The LCTs were rolling so much in the squally conditions that the commanders ignored orders to launch the Sherman 'DD' swimming tanks from 5,000 yards off-shore. Instead they crept much closer in or, in some cases, landed the Shermans directly on to the beach.

Unlike the situation on *Omaha*, very few tanks on *Gold* were lost to the sea.

The cursing, cussing groans of the first wave, laden with equipment as they charged ashore, were lost under the unmistakable, spine-chilling chirrup of Spandau

fire and the thump of mortars. But, as more and more men charged across the bullet-swept beaches, it was the Germans who found themselves on the receiving end of a sustained attack from the tanks and specialised armour from the 79th Armoured Brigade. The fore-shore was soon swarming with Crab 'flail' tanks, 'Bobbin' track-laying tanks, armoured bulldozers and all manner of mechanised assault vehicles to help the troops get up and off the beach as quickly as possible. It was on *Gold* in particular that Hobart's oft-maligned 'funnies' undoubtedly saved countless lives.

As in every battle, not everything had gone according to plan. The bombardment, heavy as it was, had failed to knock out several of the German strong points, especially at Le Hamel on the right flank where an enemy field gun was targeting the increasingly congested beach. It would take several hours of heavy fighting before an

AVRE mortar-firing tank could be brought up to suppress the position.

47 Commando Royal Marines had also been unlucky. Several of their landing craft had been destroyed at sea with heavy losses in men and equipment by the time they landed, half an hour after the first wave. Their job was to get quickly along the coast on the extreme right flank, bypassing the action at Le Hamel and behind the little resort of Arromanches-les-Bains - chosen as the site for the British Mulberry Harbour - and hopefully seize the small port of Port-en-Bassin before linking up with the Americans on *Omaha*. Despite their heavy losses, the under-strength Commando nevertheless

pressed on to its objective and, as evening fell, dug in, ready to take the port the next day.

By mid-evening Arromanches had been captured and inland the lead elements of the 50th Division had penetrated as far as the outskirts of Bayeux, and to the main road to Caen. To the east a successful link-up was made with the Canadians on *Juno* meaning that, by midnight, a substantial bridgehead six miles wide and deep had been established. The Allies here were now firmly ashore and, despite the continuing fighting, by the end of the day 24,970 troops had been landed on *Gold* with fewer than 1,000 casualties, far less than predicted.

PER MARE PER TERRAM

With a history as 'sea soldiers' that dates back 350 years, the Royal Marines have a long and proud ancestry gained through respect rather than privilege. They had fought in the days of Marlborough, had captured Gibraltar, and served in North America. They had seen bloodshed in the great 18th and 19th century sea battles, including Trafalgar. In the Great War they had suffered in the foul trenches at Gallipoli and on the Western Front.

Yet their reputation as one of the most elite Special Forces in the world, was forged more recently - in the commando and assault units created during World War II, where RM Commandos fought with distinction in Sicily, Italy, the Adriatic, and north-west Europe. In far-forgotten Burma, General - later Field Marshal - 'Bill' Slim described them as 'the finest troops in the Empire'.

And on D-Day five RM Commandos helped to spearhead the assault: 47 RM Cdo on *Gold* was assigned to link up with the Americans on *Omaha*, on *Juno* 48 RM Cdo was tasked to link up with 41 RM Cdo landing on *Sword*, where 45 RM Cdo also went ashore as part of Lord Lovat's 1st Special Service Brigade.

Meanwhile 46 RM Cdo was geared up to assault the coastal batteries in the Seine Estuary. They weren't

needed as big guns of the Royal Navy had done the job, so they landed the following day to help Canadians in the fight against the 12th SS Panzer Division *Hitlerjugend*.

Yet the Commandos were only part of the Marines' D-Day story; two-thirds of landing craft crews, including on the American beaches, were Royal Marines and their gunners manned many of the fire-support LCTs. Gun crews aboard 22 of the battleships and cruisers offshore, and half of those involved in the clearance of mines and beach obstacles were Royal Marines. Their motto - By Sea, By Land - was rarely more apt than on D-Day.

THE LIBERATION OF BAYEUX

WEDNESDAY 7 JUNE
NOTRE-DAME CATHEDRAL IN THE CENTRE OF BAYEUX

If everything had gone to plan, the citizens of Bayeux would have been 'officially' liberated a few hours earlier. The Essex Regiment and Sherwood Rangers had doggedly fought their way towards the town after landing on *Gold*, and by early evening forward patrols had entered the suburbs to rapturous acclaim. It was decided, however, that the ancient cobbled streets leading to the town centre would best be approached with care the next morning.

The wariness was unwarranted. Almost every German soldier had withdrawn, and in the early daylight hours of 7 June British tanks and infantry pushed unopposed through the cheering crowds towards the towering spires of Bayeux's magnificent gothic Notre-Dame Cathedral.

Hardly a shot had been fired.

Bayeux, with its fine buildings and long history, is one of the prettiest cities in France and was to become the centre of British operations during the Battle of Normandy. The picturesque alleys and cobbled medieval streets were, however, far too narrow and hopelessly ill-suited to the hundreds of military vehicles passing through. In an amazing feat of engineering the Royal Engineers and the Pioneer Corps hastily constructed a new road around the town - '*le by-pass*' that survives to this day.

On 14 June, the lofty unmistakable figure of General de Gaulle, Commander of the Free French, entered Bayeux to a further joyous reception to begin the establishment of his new national Free French government there.

THE LIBERATION OF BAYEUX – 7 JUNE 1944
by Simon Smith

Overlooked by the towering Notre-Dame cathedral, British Churchill tanks arrive in the centre of Bayeux to a warm welcome from flag-waving locals. The French Resistance, in a hastily painted 'Free French' Citröen, join the celebrations.

COPPS ON GOLD

Combined Operations Assault Pilotage Parties

COMBINED OPERATIONS
original drawing by Richard Taylor

Two members of the elite COPPS special operations unit paddle silently towards the shore.

FRIDAY 31 DECEMBER 1943
23.00 hours: THE BEACH AT VER-SUR-MER

It was a blustery Friday night, and the two black-clad frogmen slithered across the wet sand, hugging the ground as they went, wary of the searchlight that occasionally swept the beach around them. Ahead, beyond the foreshore, came the distant sounds of gaiety from some of the houses fronting the little seaside village of Ver-sur-Mer because this was New Year's Eve 1943 and, even in the depth of war, the German soldiers defending the coast were enjoying themselves.

The two silent figures paused for a moment as they glimpsed the dark silhouette of an idling sentry as he momentarily halted to stare out at the dark sea. Perhaps he was thinking of home far to the east, perhaps the merriment that he was missing but soon, with a sigh and deep intake of breath, he resumed his ambling patrol.

The frogmen quietly went back to work; carefully manipulating their augers into the soft ground and retrieving yet another sample of soil to fill the increasingly heavy cold metal containers slung around their rubber wetsuits.

Cautiously measuring their steps, they moved on to the next stretch, and the next, until finally they had traversed the entire beach. Creeping back to the water's edge they disappeared with their booty into the cold, rough surf to begin the tiring quarter-mile swim back to the small boat waiting to carry them out to the Royal Navy Motor Gun Boat riding the choppy swell offshore.

The samples that Major Scott-Bowden, a Royal Engineer, and Sergeant Bruce Ogden-Smith from the Commando's newly established Special Boat Section were carrying were crucial, because the beach they had just surveyed had a codename - *Gold*.

The two men were members of a small, little-known covert unit known as COPPS - Combined Operations Assault Pilotage Parties. There were less than two hundred of them, all elite soldiers trained to swim, or paddle, ashore under the cover of darkness in order to reconnoitre beaches intended for offensive landings in enemy-held territory.

For the invasion to succeed, every inch of beach was to be screened in case it was unable to support the weight of a tank or any other armoured equipment. This was another of the lessons learnt from Dieppe the previous year where much of the armour had got bogged down on the shore - easy prey to the German guns.

Within hours of Scott-Bowden and Ogden-Smith returning to England their soil samples had been rushed, under armed escort, to be analysed. The information they revealed was invaluable; in some places the sand on *Gold* covered soft patches of wet, peaty clay probably unsuitable to bear the weight of armour. Knowing this, it was now possible to plan ahead and, with the help of specialised equipment devised by the 79th Armoured Division - Hobart's Funnies - overcome the problem. The eventual success of the *Gold* landings owed much to the work of these two brave frogmen.

In the days and weeks ahead the two-man COPP teams successfully reconnoitred the other beaches, including the American *Omaha*; and if General Omar Bradley, Commander of the American First Army, didn't know it already, the detailed information that Scott-Bowden brought back to him concerning *Omaha* and its heavy defences was hardly encouraging. Scott-Bowden ended his detailed presentation to General Bradley with the prophetic words ..."and it's going to be a very tough proposition indeed, sir."

D-DAY VICTORIA CROSS

Landing with the first assault wave on *Gold* was Company Sergeant Major Stan Hollis of the 6th Battalion, The Green Howards. He had already successfully led his men off the deadly beach and was leading them towards a large battery of German guns at Mont Fleury, just inland. During the advance they encountered a German pill-box pinning his men down with machine-gun fire. In an act of extraordinary bravery, the Sergeant Major sprang up and, firing from the hip as he charged, single-handedly captured the position. A few hours later he destroyed a German field-gun.

'In the thick of it' throughout the day, CSM Hollis was awarded the only Victoria Cross awarded on D-Day. The Green Howards Museum describes his actions:

'On 6 June 1944 Company Sergeant Major Hollis was sent to ensure that two pill boxes, by-passed in the assault on the beach, were clear of enemy soldiers. When Hollis and his men were 20 yards from the pill box, a machine gun opened fire on them. Hollis instantly rushed straight at the pill box, firing his Sten gun. He jumped on top of the box, threw a grenade in through the door and fired his Sten gun into it, killing two Germans and capturing the remainder.

Later the same day Hollis attacked a field gun in Crépon, and was grazed on the right cheek by a sniper's bullet before he destroyed the gun position. Then, under fire, he diverted the enemy while two of his men who were trapped by the Germans effected their escape.'

The citation for his Victoria Cross ends with the words:

'Wherever fighting was heaviest, CSM Hollis appeared and, in the course of a magnificent day's work, he displayed the utmost gallantry and on two separate occasions his courage and initiative prevented the enemy from holding up the advance at critical stages. It was largely through his heroism and resource that the Company's objectives were gained and the casualties were not heavier: and by his own bravery, he saved the lives of many of his men."

Reproduced by kind permission of the Green Howards Museum.

THE MAPLE LEAF AT WAR

The role played by Canada during World War II is overshadowed by that of Britain across the sea, and by its mighty neighbour to the south, the USA. Yet over a million Canadians fought with great gallantry in every combat theatre of World War II - sixteen Canadians were awarded the Victoria Cross - and by the end of the war nearly three-quarters of a million men were in the Canadian Army. Materially over a half of all the Allies' supply of aluminium came from Canada, as did 90% of the nickel, and Canada built hundreds of ships and numerous aircraft, including Lancasters and Mosquitos.

Canada also provided the world's third largest navy and fourth largest air force. The contribution played by the Royal Canadian Navy to the Battle of the Atlantic was invaluable, whilst in the skies of Europe RCAF pilots had fought in France and throughout the Battle of Britain, and later provided personnel and squadrons to each of the RAF's Fighter, Bomber, Coastal and Transport Commands. By 1945 almost a quarter of Bomber Command's aircrew were from the RCAF.

On land, in 1940, the 1st Canadian Division had fought in the Battle of France, and later had battled tenaciously through the Allied invasion of Sicily and the Italian Campaign before transferring to the Netherlands in the final months of the war. In December 1941, following the Japanese attack on Pearl Harbor and the declaration of war against Japan, Canadian troops had fought in the defence of Hong Kong, refusing to surrender until, without ammunition, food or water, they were over-run on Christmas Day 1941.

In 1942 the 2nd Canadian Infantry Division had suffered so badly during the ruinous raid on Dieppe that it had to be re-built. Held in reserve on D-Day, the 2nd Division landed later and fought with distinction during the Battle of Normandy, before advancing to capture the Channel ports and into the Netherlands and north-west Germany.

On D-Day, apart from the 1st Canadian Parachute Battalion dropping with the British 6th Airborne, it fell to the 14,000 men of 3rd Canadian Infantry Division, untried in battle, to be amongst the first to land on one of the most dangerous places in the world - the beach in Normandy code-named *Juno*. They would be supported by tanks and armour of the 2nd Canadian Armoured Brigade.

THE CANADIAN LANDINGS

TUESDAY 6 JUNE
07.56 hours: JUNO BEACH

D-Day objectives: To advance inland to reach the RN13 - the main road linking Bayeux with Caen, to capture Carpiquet airfield to the west of Caen, and to link up with the British on *Gold* and *Sword* beaches.

Responsibility for the five-mile stretch of coast between the British *Sword* beach to the east and *Gold* beach to the west was given exclusively to the Canadians. The Canadian 3rd Division, supported on their left flank by 48 Commando Royal Marines, would land on the beach code-named *Juno*.

Of all five invasion beaches only *Omaha* was more difficult and dangerous, and yet on D-Day the Canadians penetrated further inland than any of the other Allied armies. In the days and weeks ahead they were also to encounter what was probably the most determined resistance from any German unit in Normandy when, just outside Caen, they met the fanatical 12th SS Panzer Division *Hitlerjugend*.

Juno, again like *Omaha*, was known to be a difficult target. The small port of Courselles-sur-Mer on the western flank was, like all ports, heavily defended, whilst in the small seaside towns of Bernières-sur-Mer and St-Aubin-sur-Mer pill boxes, bunkers and anti-tank walls stood fronting the shore alongside houses and villas heavily reinforced with concrete. In the streets behind, defensive tunnels linked strongpoints that had been built into buildings, and obstacles lined the streets; savage street-fighting would play a big part in the battle for *Juno*.

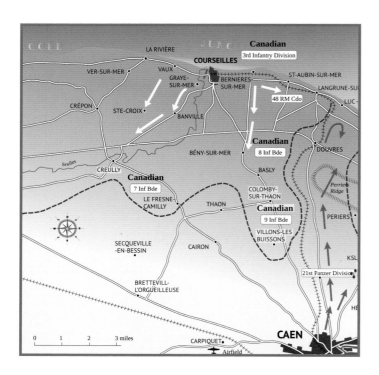

Machine-gun positions, well ranged and ready to fire, overlooked the entire beach on which minefields and barbed-wire entanglements were positioned to drive any invaders into carefully placed 'killing-zones'. Mined metal stakes lurked close under the water. The landings were going to be tough for the young Canadians and the Royal Marines.

Apart from the formidable defences, reconnaissance carried out by COPP Special Forces had identified a natural obstacle too: a rocky reef lying just offshore that, at low tide when the assault was planned, was exposed to the elements. It would therefore be impossible to land at low-water, as at all the other beaches, without the landing craft grounding offshore. Consequently the landings on *Juno* had to take place slightly later than the others.

By the time the first Canadians hit the beach at 07.56 hours, the Americans on *Utah* had been in action for almost an hour and a half, and fighting had already erupted on nearby *Gold* and *Sword*. If that wasn't enough to alert the Germans, the naval bombardment was. The defenders were under heavy shelling from the guns of HMS *Belfast* and the warships lying offshore.

As they lurched and swayed across strong off-shore currents many were violently sick, but they were at least heartened that they hadn't come under fire - yet. That was about to change. The Germans held their fire until the very last moment. Only as the first ramps hit the beach did the enemy open up, and when they did, a blizzard of fire swept the beach.

Due to the rough conditions the Sherman 'DD' tanks and the specialised Hobart 'Funnies' had, as on *Gold*, been brought closer inshore than ordered. Again, some of the LCTs landed them directly on the beach. This change of plan caused delays; instead of landing ahead of the infantry to give suppressing fire cover, the infantry landed alone and unsupported. For the first fifteen or twenty minutes they were, more or less, on their own, brutally exposed and unsupported at the mercy of the machine-gun and mortar fire sweeping relentlessly across the sands of *Juno*. Initial casualties were high.

Slowly but surely, though, as more and more armour landed, progress was made. 'Crab' flail tanks swept paths through the mines, AVREs with their deadly spigot mortars began to deal with the bunkers and pill-boxes, specialist tanks blasted apart the sea walls and bridged anti-tank ditches with fascines and ramps, and armoured bulldozers cleared paths through the wreckage. By mid-morning the streets of Bernières and Saint-Aubin had been cleared after vicious hand-to-hand fighting; the heavily-defended little port of Courseulles-sur-Mer held out a bit longer but soon the Canadians had cleared the Germans from there, too. By midday the leading units were well inland, advancing rapidly, and with the arrival of nightfall they had penetrated seven miles inland, further than any other Allied unit on 6 June.

On D-Day 21,400 troops had been landed on *Juno* beach with fewer casualties than predicted - 1,000 killed or wounded - with the majority among the unlucky few that landed first. The following day, however, the Canadians were to come face-to-face with one of the toughest German units in the whole of France - the dreaded 12th SS Panzer Division - das *Hitlerjugend*. For the Canadians a long, bitter battle against them was about to begin.

JUNO BEACH by Anthony Saunders

Ground-fire crackles below as a pair of Mk IXb Spitfires from 412 Squadron RCAF make a fast run over *Juno* beach, one of four beach patrols undertaken by the squadron on D-Day. They are supporting the 3rd Canadian Infantry Division storming ashore where, after heavy street-fighting, the small seaside town of Bernières-sur-Mer beyond the sea wall has already been cleared.

412 Squadron RCAF was one of the oldest and most illustrious units in the Royal Canadian Air Force, and formed part of the RAFs Second Tactical Air Force. Just two weeks after D-Day the entire squadron flew to its new base at the recently constructed temporary strip - officially RAF Airfield B.4 - outside the village of Bény-sur-Mer. The village lay about two miles from the coast and had been quickly liberated by the Canadians on D-Day

HMS BELFAST

Launched in 1938, the light cruiser HMS *Belfast* with her 6-inch guns was one of the most modern and powerful warships in the Royal Navy. At the outbreak of World War II she was part of the Royal Navy's Home Fleet operating out of Scapa Flow. Patrolling north of the Faroe Islands in October 1939, she came across and captured the German liner *Cap Norte*. Disguised as a liner from neutral Sweden, the liner was attempting to return to Germany from Brazil carrying, amongst others, German army reservists. The successful capture was short-lived, however, when *Belfast* struck a magnetic mine, the explosion breaking her back. After repairs and modernisation she rejoined the fleet in 1942, still the best-equipped cruiser afloat.

HMS *Belfast* then saw considerable action in the freezing waters of the Arctic where she served protecting the convoys taking supplies to Russia's northern ports of Murmansk and Archangel. At the Battle of North Cape in December 1943 she played a prominent part in the sinking of the German battle-cruiser *Scharnhorst*.

On D-Day HMS *Belfast* was part of the Eastern Naval Task Force moored between *Gold* and *Juno* beaches and was one of the first warships to open fire. With her twelve 6-inch guns triple-mounted in four turrets having a maximum range of nearly fourteen miles, she spent five weeks off the Normandy coast supporting the battles inland.

After World War II HMS *Belfast* served in the Korean War. Today, moored just upstream from Tower Bridge in London, she is part of the Imperial War Museum.

SWORD –
SECURING THE EASTERN FLANK

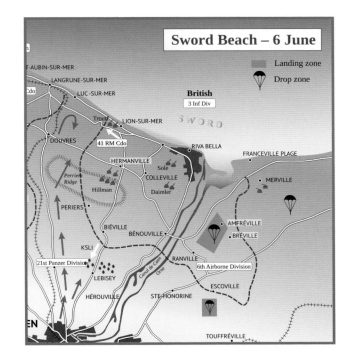

"After sailing, below deck we made a very special study of our maps, checked our arms and ammunition and had plenty of hot soup provided by one of the crew. June the 6th, soon after dawn, we were crouching low on the deck and to our left a battleship was firing, and above a few Spitfires to cover us in. At this point the enemy gunners were trying to get our range and shells were bursting all around us. Soon we were heading for our part of the Normandy coast, and at once all hell seemed to break out. As the enemy machine gunners opened up, very calmly the LCI crew dropped the landing ramps down, and with good luck from the crew we started on our way through the sea. Part of our task was to reach the airborne forces who in the night had taken and were holding the bridge, now named Pegasus Bridge. After leaving the beach we made our way through open grassland, and all around the Germans had placed notice boards warning of mines. But by a careful study of the ground we found the way across a part where cattle had been grazing some days before. We moved so fast that we were on to one group of Germans drinking coffee in the edge of a field. Our instructions had to be carried out. Push on to the bridge, never mind the odds."

W.H. Jeffries served in 6 Commando, part of Lord Lovat's 1st Special Service Brigade, and on D-Day landed on *Sword* beach from an LCI (Landing Craft Infantry)

Rupert Curtis Collection. Reproduced by kind permission of the D-Day Museum, Portsmouth

TUESDAY 6 JUNE
07.26 hours: SWORD BEACH

D-Day objectives: To advance towards Caen, and to secure the eastern flank by linking up with the British 6th Airborne Division.

Sword beach ran along the coast just to the west of the small coastal town and port of Ouistreham, where the mouth of the Orne emptied into the English Channel. The flat, sandy beach was fifty miles away from the American *Utah* and marked the eastern extremity of the D-Day landings. The task of landing here was entrusted to the British 3rd Division, veterans of Dunkirk and once commanded by General Montgomery.

Sword was well-defended; along the foreshore and close inland was a series of heavily reinforced German strongpoints, many code-named, with British quirkiness,

after fish - Cod, Trout and Sole - or the marques of well-known English cars - Hillman, Morris and Daimler. Huge field guns were also situated on the sea-front of Ouistreham and its Riva Bella casino, whilst along the coast far to the east stood a series of formidable batteries stretching all the way to Le Havre.

The successful capture of *Sword*, and the link-up with the British 6th Airborne who had landed in the early hours, was vital to secure the left flank of the entire Allied bridgehead.

At around 05.30 hours the first troops began transferring from the large landing ships into the flimsy craft that would carry them ashore. With the transports gently rolling in the swell it was an awkward and unpleasant business as tense, nervous soldiers clambered down the wet rope nets into the lurching landing craft below. By now, except for the very hardy, those who

hadn't succumbed to sea-sickness soon had as the long run-in towards the beach got under way.

Overhead the guns of the fleet spat out their thunderous bombardment, the shoreline disappearing in a maelstrom of black broiling smoke punctured by the brilliance of exploding shells. As the LCAs drew closer, a flotilla of LCT (Rockets) opened fire, drenching the beach in fire and flame as thousand-strong rocket salvos hit the beach, destroying mines, barbed wire and anything else in the vicinity. Finally, as the first enemy bullets began to spray the air, Sherman 'DD' swimming tanks and Hobart's armoured 'Funnies' wallowed ashore to engage those enemy guns still capable of firing.

At 07.26 hours the first LCAs struck the sand and lowered their ramps. Queasy yet undeterred by the murderous fire, the first troops surged ashore into the swirling morass. As on almost every beach, it was the

SWORD BEACH by Anthony Saunders

first wave who suffered the hardest losses; on *Sword* that dubious honour fell to units of the British 8th Infantry Brigade but, displaying exceptional courage and determination, and supported by the armour, they forced their way across the savage shore.

At 07.50 hours the Royal Marines of 41 Commando landed together with 4 Army Commando, and with them 177 Free French commandos selected from the 1st Fusiliers Marins. They were the first of their countrymen to land on their native soil and, under the command of Capitaine Philippe Kieffer, fought with bravery and distinction in the capture of the Riva Bella casino strongpoint. The Royal Marines headed west to deal with 'Trout' and attempted to link up with 48 Royal Marines Commando heading their way from *Juno*.

Meanwhile Lord Lovat's 1st Special Service Brigade swept inland, fighting as they went, towards the airborne forces holding out at Pegasus Bridge. They successfully linked up with the 6th Airborne shortly after 13.00 hours with the bizarre sight of Lord Lovat's personal piper, Billy Millen, kilt swirling, playing at their head. It wasn't the only curious scene that day; as the battle raged around them, most locals kept their heads safely down but at Colleville-sur-Orne, the British were surprised to be greeted by the sight of the village Mayor appearing like an apparition through the swirling smoke, proudly wearing a gleaming fireman's helmet, highly polished for the occasion.

Apart from some congestion on the beach caused by the fast-rising tide, the attack, although bitter and bloody, was proceeding well. During the afternoon, however, the Germans finally counter-attacked. The 21st Panzer Division had been switched from attacking the British airborne forces to thrust deep into the gap that existed between *Sword* and the Canadians on *Juno*. Although the attack was repulsed, the Panzers had succeeded in stalling the British advance; by midnight, despite the fact that 28,845 British troops had been landed on *Sword*, and with casualties of less than 1,000, they came to a halt still some three miles short of their objective - Caen - a name that would come to haunt them in the weeks ahead.

During the afternoon of D-Day Hitler finally consented to the deployment of his beloved 12th SS Panzer Division *Hitlerjugend*. By the morning of 7 June these fanatical SS troops had quickly manoeuvred themselves into position between Caen and the Allies. It would take many days, and many lives, to cover those three bloody miles; Caen would not finally fall until 18 July.

OLD LADIES AND BATTERIES

Apart from the Merville battery - which directly overlooked *Sword* and whose destruction had been entrusted to 9 Para - there were big concerns about the coastal batteries strategically sited along the coast between the mouth of the Orne at Ouistreham and the port of Le Havre, where the Seine spills into the Channel. Overlooking the sea-lanes that the *Sword* invasion fleet must take, each of these positions was equipped with 155mm (6-inch) guns, protected by reinforced concrete casements.

The task of obliterating the largest of the sites was given to two elderly but still powerful Royal Navy battleships, both armed with eight massive 15-inch guns: HMS *Warspite* - nicknamed *The Grand Old Lady* - had seen action at the Battle of Jutland during World War I and during her career had earned more battle honours than any other ship in the Royal Navy, and HMS *Ramillies*, also a veteran of the Great War and who, on 6 June and the days following, is reckoned to have fired more than a thousand 15-inch shells, more than any other warship. Joining them was the monitor HMS *Roberts* with her twin 15-inch guns.

Whilst the guns on shore were being eliminated, however, a small flotilla of German E-boats had slipped out of Le Havre unnoticed through the smoke screen laid

to cover the fleet's position. They just had time to deliver a fan of torpedoes before making a hurried withdrawal. One torpedo, by chance, hit the Norwegian destroyer *Svenner*, splitting her in two and sending her to the bottom.

Amongst the other naval warships bombarding the beach defences was the Polish-manned 6-inch cruiser ORP *Dragon*. Formerly the Royal Navy's HMS *Dragon*, the ship had been handed over to the Polish Navy at the beginning of 1943. On 8 July, a month after D-Day, *Dragon* was preparing to shell targets around Caen when she was attacked and badly damaged by that rarest of weapons, a German human-torpedo, leading to her being scuttled to form a breakwater to the British Mulberry harbour.

SAINTE CROIX-SUR-MER

CANADIAN WING by Robert Taylor

Flying from their base at Ford in West Sussex, Mk IX Spitfires of 'Johnnie' Johnson's Canadian Wing, complete with newly painted 'invasion' markings, make a sweep above the beaches on D-Day. Four days later they will transfer to Sainte Croix-sur-Mer.

With gunfire still less than a mile away, no sooner had the Canadians cleared the little village of Sainte Croix-sur-Mer of Germans than the first Sappers and Pioneers arrived. The village lay just inland from the junction of *Gold* and *Juno* beaches, and within a matter of hours advance units of the Royal Engineers Airfield Construction Group were hard at work surveying the site, known to them as ALG B.3 - Advanced Landing Ground B.3 Sainte Croix-sur-Mer. What was now fields of ripening wheat were about to be transformed into the first temporary airstrip in liberated France.

Soon the first bulldozers were lumbering up from the beach, followed swiftly by graders as the job of levelling the site got underway. Then the heavy trucks arrived, sagging under the weight of the Somerfield tracking - wire mesh wound into rolls to form the new 3,600 foot long runway. The trucks would deliver hundreds of tons of it, all to be unwound by hand. The bare earth was then to be re-sown, the crates of grass seed looking somewhat incongruous beside the stack of engineering equipment.

A basic dispersal area was constructed, huts appeared, and the ground crew started to arrive, fitters, mechanics, electricians, carpenters and cooks. A canteen went up, tents were erected and 'facilities' dug. Thousands of 'Jerry-cans' were unloaded and man-handled into a nearby fuel dump, along with tons of ammunition. Spare parts arrived and were stored. It was a mammoth task but, just four days after the first troops had stormed ashore, the new landing strip was ready for use.

On the morning of 10 June 1944 the familiar sound of Merlin engines was heard over Sainte Croix-sur-Mer. The first of the Spitfires lowered its wheels and touched down, quickly followed by the rest. Johnnie Johnson and his 144 Canadian Wing had arrived.

ST CROIX-SUR-MER by Robert Taylor

Top Ace Johnnie Johnson and his famous 144 Canadian Wing scramble from the newly prepared airstrip at Sainte Croix-sur- Mer for the RAF's first combat sweep from French soil after D-Day.

WELCOME RESPITE by Richard Taylor

TOWARDS CARENTAN

Carentan was a pivotal hub: from the north the RN13 - Napoleon's great imperial highway linking Cherbourg to the gates of Paris - approached the town across a mile-long causeway built above nature's floodplain of the River Douve. This area had been deliberately flooded by the Germans who had opened the tidal lock on the river at La Barquette, north of the town.

To the east the main road headed towards Bayeux and Caen. Other roads radiated out across the Cotentin, south towards Brittany and inland towards Saint-Lô, as did the railway.

Geography, therefore, had made Carentan a prosperous market town, and the strategic importance of its location was not lost on either the Allies or the Germans. If the Americans were to link up their two bridgeheads of *Utah* and *Omaha* and advance across the Cotentin peninsula and north to capture Cherbourg, Carentan had to be taken quickly. To secure the town, the Americans first had to seize the causeway, with its bridges over the Douve.

The Americans faced stiff resistance. Fighting a determined, often brutal, rear-guard action, the élite German paratroopers from 2nd Fallschirmjäger Division had, however, been finally pushed back and had withdrawn into the town. They were commanded by a battle-hardened veteran, Oberstleutnant Friedrich von der Heydte, recently awarded the Oak Leaves to the Knight's Cross he had been given during the invasion of Crete. Heydte had been ordered to hold the town 'at all costs'.

STAND EASY by Simon Smith

During a short respite from the heavy fighting on D-Day, paratroopers from the 101st Airborne stand easy outside a recently liberated café as they await orders to advance towards their next objective - Carentan.

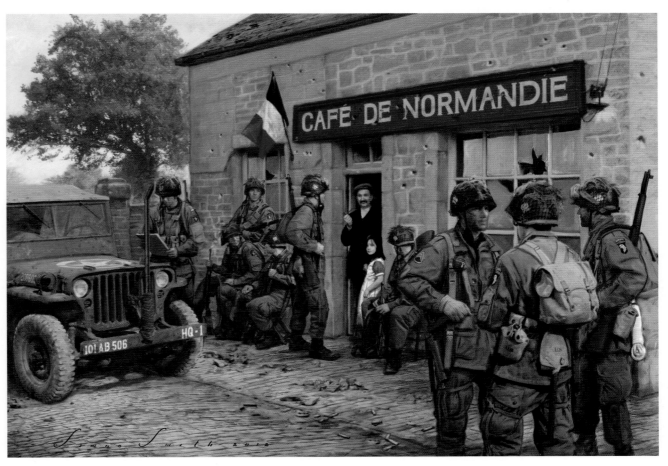

Detail from an original pencil drawing by Richard Taylor.

The fighting in the villages behind *Utah* beach has diminished. With their jeeps ready to go, American paratroopers from the 101st Airborne wait for the order to move against Carentan.

DEAD MAN'S CORNER

WEDNESDAY 7 JUNE

Utah beach was out on a limb, separated from *Omaha* to the east by the broad shallow estuary where Carentan stood at the head. Bordered by the *marais* - an impassable marshy foreshore that shifted with the changing tide - this was a place more suited to migrating birds than invading armies, especially one with tanks.

The only way the Americans could link *Utah* to *Omaha* was through Carentan. The task of seizing it fell to the 101st Airborne.

The road along which the tanks from *Utah* must pass to get to Carentan was small, a country lane that began as no more than a coarse track that led inland through the sandy dunes towards the village of Sainte-Marie-du-Mont, captured by the 101st on D-Day. From here the narrow lane headed inland towards the neighbouring Saint-Côme-du-Mont where, on the south side of the village, it joined the main RN13 just above the causeway that ran into Carentan a mile or so away.

At any other time it could have been a beautiful lane bordered by hedge-bound fields where cattle grazed amiably, unconcerned and unaware of the paratroopers who, less than thirty-six hours earlier and in the dead of night, had landed amongst them. There were brimming orchards, full of shortly to ripen apples and pears. Wildflowers scented the air. But nature's tranquillity was just an illusion as the men of the 501st Parachute Infantry Regiment crept slowly forward towards Saint-Côme-du-Mont. Enemy snipers had hindered them all the way until the first, recently-landed tanks appeared on the scene in support.

Approaching the crossroads, a blizzard of machine-gun fire opened up on them from German Fallschirmjägers hidden and well-entrenched around the elegant stone house that stood nearby. Almost immediately the lead tank - a Stuart Mk3 - was hit by a *panzerfaust* anti-tank grenade, instantly killing the crew. Late in the evening the Americans withdrew to re-group for a fresh assault at dawn, leaving the unfortunate tank commander hanging unceremoniously out of the turret.

DEAD MAN'S CORNER by Simon Smith

THURSDAY 8 JUNE

Reinforced to three battalions, the assault on Saint-Côme-du-Mont began with a creeping artillery barrage, the position at the crossroads being described simply as 'the corner with the dead guy in the tank'. Later it was named 'Dead Man's Corner'.

In a swirl of savage fighting the 101st swept into the village, forcing the Germans back and clearing 'Dead Man's Corner' despite relentless counter-attacks. Finally the Germans withdrew back across the causeway. Oberstleutnant von der Heydte and his Fallschirmjägers would make their stand in Carentan.

Now all the 101st had to do was cross the causeway and take the town…

THE TAKING OF CARENTAN

SATURDAY 10 JUNE

The causeway into Carentan from Saint-Côme-du-Mont had been built decades ago, constructed by the townsfolk to keep the main road well above the floodplain of the two rivers that flowed to the north of the town. On either side of the high embankment, and the four bridges that spanned the rivers and their tributaries, lay marshland and the flooded fields that were now impassable to all. If it had been built as a defence for times of war, rather than against the elements, then it couldn't have been better designed. To capture it the 101st would have to cross it in the old-fashioned way - on foot.

The tough Fallschirmjägers, however, smarting from withdrawal, intended to stop them by any means possible.

Under savage mortar and machine-gun fire the 502nd Parachute Infantry Regiment advanced, dashing forward man by man, yard by yard, taking whatever cover they could find. Constant sniper-fire pinged around them, and throughout the night flares lit the sky, determined to reveal the battered Americans as they crept on. By dawn on 11 June, the 502nd had reached the final bridge where they were pinned down by withering fire coming from around a large, fortified stone farmhouse nearby. Unable to silence it by an artillery barrage, Lieutenant-Colonel

Cole ordered his men to fix bayonets and, leading from the front, charged in a full frontal attack. The hand-to-hand combat that followed was bloody and brutal but the positions were taken and, despite aggressive counter-attacks, held. The charge had won the battle for which Cole was awarded the Medal of Honor.

During the evening Oberstleutnant von der Heydte ordered his weary Fallschirmjägers to withdraw; they were down to their last rounds of ammunition. Further defence was pointless. The 502nd PIR, too, were exhausted.

$\longrightarrow$

EASY COMPANY - THE TAKING OF CARENTAN by Chris Collingwood

The men of *Easy* Company 2nd Battalion 506th PIR face the enemy in close combat, corner-to-corner street fighting as they battle against the German rearguard in Carentan.

EASY COMPANY - MOVING ON by Chris Collingwood

Major Dick Winters and the men of *Easy* Company take up a holding position in Carentan after the capture of the town. It's a brief but welcome respite from the bitter hand-to hand fighting they have just endured.

MONDAY 12 JUNE

Dawn broke over the causeway to reveal that the Fallschirmjägers had pulled out. As the 101st entered Carentan, however, they came under heavy machine-gun fire from the German rearguard covering the withdrawal. As German artillery positions on high ground to the south, still in enemy hands, lobbed shells amongst them the men of the 506th PIR fought their way through to the town centre in a series of gruesome fire-fights. And then it was over. What was left of the German rearguard melted away as best it could.

Unknown to von der Heydte, however, elements of the 17th SS Panzergrenadier Division *Götz von Berlichingen* had been advancing north towards Carentan. Linking up with the withdrawing Fallschirmjägers they quickly counter-attacked the town, pushing back and nearly overwhelming the 101st holding the defensive perimeter. For a moment the situation was critical but *Easy* Company of the 506th PIR, and others from 502nd PIR, stood their ground in a valiant defence, allowing just enough time for advancing American tanks from the US 2nd Armored Division to arrive and repulse the German thrust.

The Battle of Carentan was finally over, but the battle for Normandy had only just begun....

Original pencil drawing by Richard Taylor.

Original pencil drawing by Richard Taylor

HOLDING THE LINE

TUESDAY 13 JUNE

VILLIERS-BOCAGE

Dusk was falling as the muddy Tiger tanks arrived outside the small town of Villiers-Bocage. It was 12 June and they had been travelling for five days, ever since Hitler had stopped prevaricating and ordered their advance north from their reserve position at Beauvais.

The Tigers, part of SS-Panzer-Abteilung 101, were commanded by SS-Hauptsturmführer Michael Wittmann, a legendary veteran of Kursk and one of the most successful Panzer commanders on the Eastern Front. Awarded the Knight's Cross with Oak Leaves, he had already destroyed well over a hundred Soviet tanks, as well as numerous vehicles and artillery pieces.

The following morning a squadron of British Cromwell tanks from the 22nd Armoured Division advanced into the town, unaware of the hidden Tigers. Wittman seized the moment and opened fire.

Surprised and out-classed by the heavily-armoured Tiger MkVI, there could only be one winner. One Cromwell after another fell victim to the Tiger's 88mm gun and, as Wittmann thundered through the town, tanks and Bren-gun carriers were blasted apart. Within a quarter of an hour he and his small force had knocked out 14 British tanks, a couple of Bren-gun carriers and an equally large haul of vehicles.

Hitler was delighted by Wittmann's impressive victory at Villiers-Bocage, awarding him Swords to his Knight's Cross. The triumph, however, was short-lived. On 8 August, just south of Caen, the gunner of a Sherman Firefly equipped with its powerful 17-pounder anti-tank gun, got a Tiger in his sights, and fired.

The Tiger exploded, it was Wittmann's. The celebrated Panzer Ace was dead.

HOLDING THE LINE by Richard Taylor

Mk VI Tiger heavy tanks from SS-Panzer-Abteilung 101 pass through a small hamlet in Normandy as they head north towards the front line. The area has seen recent fighting and a wrecked German half-track armoured personnel carrier still smoulders beside the road.

The Tigers, for once, have temporary air cover. Two Messerschmitt Bf109s race overhead but they won't be around for long: Allied air supremacy in the area is far too strong for the depleted Luftwaffe.

INTO THE BOCAGE

There was nothing quite like the *bocage*. In peacetime it was an enchanted landscape where narrow sunken lanes meandered past a network of little orchards. Haphazard pastures lay bordered by dense tangled hedges, growing out from high earth banks constructed and cultivated over centuries to serve as protection against the elements; in many ways similar to Devon.

Twice a day, regular as clockwork, cattle ambled leisurely along the rutted tracks to be milked, passing stone farmhouses and isolated barns in scenes unchanged over the generations. It was the gentle ebb and flow of the seasons that governed the pace of life in the *bocage* until, in June 1944, war paid its brief visit. It turned heaven into hell.

No one was prepared for the *bocage*. No one had trained for it, and few had fought in anything like it. The veteran General, 'Lightning' Joe Collins, who commanded the US VII Corps, said that fighting through bocage country was 'worse than anything he had encountered in the jungles of Guadalcanal'. But, with the flanks now secured by the Airborne Divisions, if the Allies wanted to break out across Normandy, they had no choice but to fight their way through it.

For the German defenders the *bocage* was perfect countryside in which to practise the dark arts of ambush and surprise. It was impossible for any attacker to see beyond the next thicket, each corner and every field a potential battle-ground. Hedgerows provided the perfect background in which to conceal a machine-gun,

or camouflage a sniper. It was a place where the single crack of an assassin's rifle, unheard by its victim, broke the excruciating tension as, platoon by platoon, small groups of edgy soldiers fought grimly from hedgerow to hedgerow.

The high-shouldered lanes were almost impassable to tanks; a well-sited anti-tank gun could instantly turn any of them into a killing-zone. There was no escape. In places the steep earth banks, especially when it rained - which it often did - resembled the parapets of First World War trenches, and the carnage associated with them.

Farms became fortresses, barns strong-points. The Germans, courtesy of their experience in the harsh realities of the Eastern Front, had learnt every trick in the field-craft manual. They now unleashed those hard-won

Drawing by Simon Smith

skills against the Allies, many of whom were, as yet, untested in battle.

And above this leafy maze hung the sickly stench of death as the bloated corpses of dead cattle decayed in the summer air.

Some men cracked in the *bocage*, they couldn't take any more. Many more died but steadily, just as had happened on the shores of *Omaha*, individuals and tenacious small groups showed an uncanny ability to adapt to the conditions. Painfully the Allied armies learnt how to deal with the Germans, and by mid-July the Americans finally broke through in the west.

In the east, where the Germans had expected the Allies' main thrust to come from, the British 2nd Army, who had borne the brunt of the German counter-attack, were slowly winning the bitter war of attrition. On 18 July what remained of Caen finally fell, the Canadians overcoming the last pockets of resistance held by the 12th SS Panzer Division.

Whilst the British were fighting their way through the German Panzers towards Villiers-Bocage, the Americans were rapidly swinging around from the south. What was left of the German 7th Army was quickly being bottled up - and the bottle-neck was a place called Falaise.

MONDAY 17 JULY
SAINTE-FOY-DE-MONTGOMMERY

With Caen doomed and the German Army facing increasing pressure, command of Army Group B was thrown into further confusion. On 17 July its commander, the legendary Erwin Rommel, was badly wounded. He was returning from a visit to the headquarters of 1 SS Panzer Corps when his car was spotted from above by the pilot of a patrolling Spitfire from 602 Squadron. They were close to the aptly named village of Sainte-Foy-de-Montgommery.

The driver of the staff car had also spotted the Spitfire. With his foot flat down on the accelerator he frantically increased speed as the sleek little fighter swooped from behind, 20mm cannon shells chasing the car in an unequal battle of speed. A shell tore through the driver's arm and the big Mercedes careered off the road, crashing into the trees.

Rommel escaped with his life but not without cost. He had severe wounds to his head and was hospitalised. Three days later, unknown to Rommel, a plot to assassinate the increasingly paranoid Hitler failed.

Rommel, once the great hero of Germany, was implicated and forced, to save his reputation and his family's lives, to commit suicide.

Günther von Kluge now took over command of Army Group B as well as that of his own as the newly-appointed overall Commander-in-Chief (West).

Rommel an original pencil drawing by Richard Taylor

Original pencil drawings by Robert Taylor.

Original pencil drawing
by Richard Taylor

THE TRAGEDY OF CAEN

SUNDAY 9 JULY

Hitler was apoplectic with rage - Cherbourg had surrendered. Despite his personal order that it be defended to the last man, on 26 June a white flag flew over the remains of the garrison overlooking the town. It was the end; two days later the commander of the harbour defences also surrendered.

With Cherbourg and the Cotentin lost, Rommel and the German Army generals had urged the Führer to withdraw to a more easily-defended line along the east bank of the Orne. The mere thought of surrendering Caen sent Hitler into a tirade, screaming abuse about the 'defeatism' of his officers. The order was given that Caen - like Stalingrad - was never to surrender.

If only Montgomery could have captured Caen on D-Day, because no one accepted Hitler's new order with more relish than the SS Panzer Divisions.

Caen, as at Stalingrad, held out for a month. The 12th SS Panzer Division in particular fought with increasing levels of vicious defiance but, for the historic city, the tragedy was still to come. On the night of 7 July a large force of Lancaster and Halifax heavy bombers attacked, Caen was obliterated. Where once had stood a magnificent city, now lay ruins.

The Germans, though, had had enough; whilst wisps of smoke rose from the still-smouldering rubble, the British and Canadians advanced through the desolate streets. By 9 July most of Caen was at last in Allied hands. Only in the southern suburbs did the fanatical 12th SS Panzer Grenadiers made one last, defiant stand. They held out for over a week and then it was all over - Caen had fallen.

The battle had been long; it had seen some of the bitterest fighting of the war. But the British and Canadians had taken on the best troops in the German Army.

And they had won.

CLOSE QUARTERS by Simon Smith

A Panther tank, destroyed by Canadians from the Regina
Rifle Regiment using a hand-held PIAT anti-tank gun, lies
wrecked in the streets of Bretteville-l'Orgueilleuse, a few
miles from the eastern suburbs of Caen, 9 June 1944. It
would take a month of fierce and bitter fighting for the
British and Canadians to liberate the city.

ROLLING THUNDER

an original pencil drawing by Richard Taylor

Already badly damaged by Allied bombing, Alencon was the
scene of bitter fighting as General George Patton's US 3rd
Army hooked round from the south to cut off the Falaise
pocket. The Americans faced stiff resistance from the 9th
Panzer Division and the 2nd SS-Panzer Division *Das Reich*,
before finally liberating the city on 20 August.

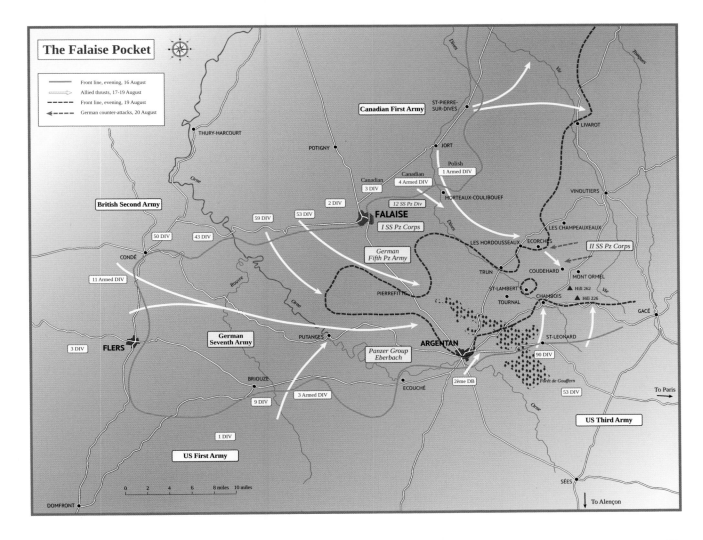

The Falaise Pocket

- Front line, evening, 16 August
- Allied thrusts, 17-19 August
- Front line, evening, 19 August
- German counter-attacks, 20 August

FALAISE - CLOSING THE GAP

MONDAY 21 AUGUST

As the Allies advanced, Hitler - delusional as ever - ordered his Panzers to counter-attack and throw the enemy back to the sea rather than allow retreat. But attack with what? The German 7th Army was already in turmoil.

Somehow, a few under-strength Panzer Divisions were assembled but, for all of Hitler's dreams of past glories, the Allies possessed a secret of their own. Thanks to the code-breakers at Bletchley Park the German plans were intercepted and when the Panzers made their move,

the Allies were ready and waiting. Within a couple of days the last major German counter-attack in Normandy was over. The Panzers, together with the rest of the German 7th Army, now found itself in danger of being encircled.

The newly-activated American 3rd Army, commanded by the mercurial, gun-slinging General George S. Patton, was sweeping rapidly across the countryside, south of the Germans. If they continued at the rate they were going it would only be a matter of days,

if not hours, before they linked up with the Canadians and the 1st Polish Armoured Division who were furiously thrusting down from the north towards the town of Falaise. As the British 2nd Army and American 1st Army squeezed from the west and north-west, the pocket was constricting and the noose growing tighter.

Hitler was beside himself with fury, blaming the *débacle* on Generalfeldmarschall Günther von Kluge, who had succeeded von Rundstedt as Commander-in-Chief (West). On 17 August the Führer sacked

CLOSING THE GAP by Robert Taylor

Hawker Typhoon Mk.Ib fighter-bombers from 247 Squadron
RAF make a rapid exit from the target area close to Falaise.
With engines racing at full throttle, the distant scenes of
havoc wreaked in their wake bear witness to the devastation
of their powerful rockets. Fuel and ammunition from a
retreating German column explode skywards with shattering
detonations, tongues of fire erupting within the churning
black smoke.

von Kluge who, disgraced and believing the war now lost, committed suicide.

By now, in the German 7th Army, the situation was chaotic as every man fled before the onslaught, leaving almost all of their armour and equipment behind. Allied aircraft and artillery pounded them relentlessly yet many, too many, escaped the net and retreated headlong towards the Seine. Most, however, were trapped. On Monday 21 August the Canadians and Poles sealed the last escape route out of the pocket and the pugnacious-looking, rocket-firing Typhoons of the RAF's Second Tactical Air Force began to deconstruct what remained of the German 7th Army.

Preceded by the distinctive whine of their Sabre engines, the Typhoons unleashed their deadly fire-power on to the massed columns of German vehicles and armour trapped within the pocket below. By the time the Typhoons had finished, little could compare to the nightmare of destruction they had inflicted, other than a scene from hell itself. Thousands of shattered and burning vehicles and tanks blocked every road; incinerated corpses of men, and horses, lay charred and rotting amongst the mangled remains. Once green fields now lay torn apart, strewn with the débris of a broken army. The putrid reek of death fouled the air.

For the German Army Falaise was more than a humiliating rout, it was a catastrophe. They were broken and in retreat. The Battle for Normandy was over, Allied troops entered Paris on 25 August - and two weeks later they were approaching the German border.

Original pencil drawing by Robert Taylor

TYPHOONS OUTWARD BOUND by Richard Taylor

OVERLORD

– 6 JUNE 1944 –

D-DAY AND THE BATTLE FOR NORMANDY

PART II

WINGS OF VICTORY

WARBIRDS IN NORMANDY

PAINTINGS FROM THE MILITARY GALLERY

DAWN TILL DUSK by Richard Taylor

Fighter Ace Johnnie Johnson leads Mk.IX Spitfires of his 144
Canadian Wing back to their base at Ford after a long day of
operations over Normandy shortly after D-Day.

PART II

WINGS OF VICTORY

In June 1940 the Germans were poised to invade Britain. The only thing stopping them was the RAF. Without total air supremacy the landing barges, massed in Boulogne and the other Channel ports, would be bombed into oblivion well before a single Panzer could land. The invasion failed because the Luftwaffe was unable to defeat Fighter Command in the Battle of Britain.

In June 1944 it was the Allies preparing to invade, and the Luftwaffe was but a mere shadow of the force it had once been. Many of their top pilots were gone; with young, inexperienced and quickly-trained replacements stepping into their shoes. Production of aircraft had slowed to a trickle, with the factories pummelled by Bomber Command at night and the Americans by day. In June 1944, total air supremacy was in Allied hands.

The paintings in this collection are not definitive of every type of aircraft involved on D-Day or in the battle for Normandy. B-17s and B-24s, for example, carried out numerous bombing missions before, during and after the invasion. It does, however, portray just a hint of the wide variety of aircraft that did take part. And some - like the Typhoon - that the Battle of Normandy turned into legends.

WARBIRDS IN NORMANDY
PAINTINGS FROM THE MILITARY GALLERY

DOUGLAS
C-47 DAKOTA
THE FINEST TRANSPORT OF WORLD WAR II

In the middle of the afternoon on 17 December 1935, a new aircraft taxied away from the Douglas plant in Santa Monica, and on to the runway. Carl Cover, the test pilot that day, made one last check, then pushed down the throttles as far as they would go. The big Wright Cyclone radial engines responded immediately. Quickly gathering speed, the rear wheel gently lifted and, moments later,

the machine was airborne. It was the maiden flight of the new, beautiful-looking Douglas DC-3.

With a carrying capacity twice that of its Boeing rival, the new airliner was an instant commercial hit. Soon DC-3s were equipping every major airline in America and selling overseas. With the outbreak of war in Europe, the U.S. Army Air Corps took note; in September 1940 they

ordered over 500 DC-3s adapted for military use. They were the first of many because, by the end of the war, more than 10,000 had been built.

Doing away with such niceties as panelling, the seats were stripped out and replaced with crude benches along the sides. A large loading door was added and the floor and rear fuselage section strengthened to carry heavy loads. The rugged new version was called the C-47 Skytrain.

C-47s became the military workhorse of the war, forming the backbone of every Allied air force and serving in every combat theatre around the world. They hauled cargo, could carry a jeep, light guns and transported passengers. They towed troop-carrying gliders and dropped paratroopers; a C-47 could handle up to a maximum of 22 fully equipped men. They evacuated casualties and stretcher cases, flew covert missions and collected agents behind enemy lines. The Russians manufactured over 2,000 of them under licence; some versions equipped with skis operated on the snow-clad Eastern Front. In the RAF the C-47 was known as the Dakota, and that was the name that went around the world.

Even the enemy used them. The Japanese, who had acquired a licence to build the DC-3 before the war, called them the Shōwa L2D, code-named 'Tabby' by the

INTO BATTLE by Robert Taylor

As white parachutes litter the sky, US airborne troops jump into battle from their C-47 Dakotas, inland from *Utah* beach on D-Day. Each C-47 usually carried a "stick" of between 18 and 20 paratroopers.

THE ROAD TO THE RHINE by Robert Taylor

Three months after they had dropped on D-Day the US 82nd and 101st Airborne Divisions, this time alongside the British 1st Airborne Division and Polish 1st Parachute Brigade, were called into action again. And so were the C-47s and their crews. On 17 September 1944, they took part in *Operation Market Garden,* the attempt to seize six bridges over the Rhine. It was the largest airborne assault ever undertaken.

Allies. The L2D was the most important transport plane in the Japanese air force.

For a paratrooper, however, getting on board was not the easiest task in the book. The cockpit, just ahead of the cabin, stands about 25 feet off the ground, the fuselage sloping steeply back to the rear. Not only did the paratroopers have to climb on board - not easy for anyone with a parachute, let alone someone also carrying his weapon, ammunition, equipment and the extra supplies needed for the first days - but they were then faced with a stiff climb, clawing their way up inside. Last on, first out was probably best!

There is no doubt of the heroic role played by C-47s in the Normandy invasion and subsequent battle. On D-Day over 800 C-47s carried the 82nd and 101st US Airborne Divisions to the Cotentin, whilst others from the RAF's 46 Group ferried the British 6th Airborne to their drop zones around the Orne. Within the first 72 hours C-47s had carried over 50,000 airborne troops across the Channel to France.

RAF DAKOTA

The RAF called the C-47 the Dakota. Not after the place in North America, but the company that built them - DACoTA - Douglas Aircraft Company Transport Aircraft.

More than 2,000 RAF Dakotas served with distinction during the war, especially in Burma: in May 1942 a single Dakota from 31 Squadron carried 65 people to safety from the advancing Japanese - and at D-Day and the subsequent *Operation Market Garden* at Arnhem.

THE GLIDER TUGS
HANDLEY PAGE

HALIFAX A.Mk.III

Seemingly destined to be forever overshadowed by its illustrious counterpart in Bomber Command - the Avro Lancaster - the Handley Page Halifax nevertheless equally shouldered much of the hard work. By the end of the war it had developed into a formidable, hard-working bomber, equipping numerous units that included RAF, Canadian, Australian, Free French and Polish squadrons.

Its first operational mission, on the night of 11 / 12 March 1942, was to bomb harbour facilities at Le Havre. Two years later they would return to Normandy again, this time as tugs, towing a vast armada of gliders. It was just one of the many and varied roles for which the Halifax was adapted.

It was used as a ferry for covert SOE operations - the only aircraft with a long enough range to carry SOE agents, weapons and equipment to eastern Europe. In June 1942 a Halifax from 138 (Special Duties) Squadron dropped the British trained Czech soldiers who assassinated Reinhard Heydrich, an architect of the Holocaust and Deputy *Reichsprotektor*, in Prague.

In July 1943 Halifaxes towed Horsa gliders for the first time in combat during *Operation Husky* - the Allied invasion of Sicily - but it was in northern France, on D-Day, that the Halifax earned its formidable reputation as a tug. It was one of the few aircraft with the power and strength to tow the massive, tank-carrying Hamilcar glider. Later, during the airborne operations in Holland, and in the Rhine crossings, the Halifax tugs once again lived up to their hard-won fame.

An original drawing
by Robert Taylor

SHORT
STIRLING Mk.IV

The Stirling might have been the first four-engined monoplane bomber in the RAF, but it certainly wasn't the most glamorous, despite the fact that its design was an evolution of Short's beautiful Sunderland flying-boat. Shorts had cleverly modified the design, removed the hull and added wheels. The new aircraft did have its quirky attractions, though; a high bubble cockpit sitting on top of the long fuselage gave it the appearance of a flying goose - minus the beak!

Crucially, however, Shorts had had to remove over 12 feet from the Sunderland's original wingspan to conform to the Air Ministry's new specification. The result was a lack of lift from which the Stirling would

always suffer. The tall, gangly undercarriage, designed to tilt the airframe back to assist on take-off, became one of the most distinctive sights in Bomber Command. But, of more importance at the time, the Stirling could carry a much greater bomb-load further than its predecessors - aircraft such as the Whitley.

By 1943 the Stirling was past its prime and had begun to be withdrawn from front-line service with Bomber Command. But it wasn't the end: the Stirling was to be resurrected as a glider-tug and transport. Arguably, some of its finest moments were still to come.

On 6 June 1944, the newly revitalised Stirlings - the Mk.IV - flew more than 200 sorties with 38 Group RAF,

dropping paratroopers and towing Horsa gliders for the British 6th Airborne Division. Stirlings of 218 Squadron also took part in *Operation Glimmer*, the precision dropping of 'window' - thin strips of metal - designed to confuse German radar operators into thinking that an invasion fleet was steaming at a steady 8 knots towards the Pas de Calais.

The Stirling Mk.IVs went on to perform with great credit at Arnhem and, in March 1945, were still going strong when they participated in *Operation Varsity* - the crossing of the river Rhine.

ARMSTRONG WHITWORTH
A.W.41 ALBEMARLE

Conceived for one role, and used for another: that was the story of Armstrong Whitworth's unremarkable Albemarle. Intended as a twin-engined, reconnaissance bomber, it was to be largely assembled from pre-fabricated parts, using wood and steel, then covered with a plywood skin. It was a far cheaper method than using expensive alloys. In small factories up and down the country, hundreds of sub-contractors went to work, but getting the supply chain to work efficiently proved time-consuming.

Although the first prototype had flown in March 1940, the delays in production meant that it was nearly two years later, in December 1941, that the first complete Albemarles were rolling out of the factory. It wasn't a bad-looking aircraft - its new, tricycle undercarriage setting it apart - but by now, because of the delays, there were other, better, aircraft coming on stream.

Even though they undertook a couple of bombing sorties, the decision had already been made to change its role into that of a glider tug.

In July 1943 the Albemarle tugs went into battle for the first time, towing gliders during the invasion of Sicily. On D-Day they were in the thick of the action again, this time dropping the airborne Pathfinders in the early hours of 6 June before four squadrons of Albemarle's began towing Horsas to Normandy.

Their swansong came at Arnhem, after which they were withdrawn from front-line service. The 600 Albemarles that had been built could never be described as 'great' or 'classic' aircraft, yet neither were they a failure.. When the time came, in the new role they were tasked to perform, they carried out their duties competently and without fuss. The ordinary Albemarle served its country extraordinarily well.

An original drawing
by Richard Taylor

ROLL OF HONOUR

An original drawing by Richard Taylor depicting the remains of a Horsa glider that landed near the town of Wesel during *Operation Varsity* on 24 March 1945.

Horsa gliders took part in every major airborne assault:

OPERATION FRESHMAN - 19 NOVEMBER 1942: The unsuccessful attack on the German heavy water plant in Norway. 23 survivors from two crashed Horsas were executed on Hitler's order.

OPERATION HUSKY - 10 JULY 1943: The invasion of Sicily.

OPERATION OVERLORD - 6 JUNE 1944: The invasion of Normandy.

OPERATION DRAGOON - 15 AUGUST 1944: The invasion of southern France

OPERATION VARSITY - 24 MARCH 1945: The Rhine crossings.

AIRSPEED
HORSA GLIDER
THE 'OTHER' WOODEN WONDER

Mention a wartime aircraft built out of wood and most people will think of the de Havilland Mosquito, affectionately known as 'the Wooden Wonder'. There was, however, another of equal merit - the Airspeed Horsa.

There was nothing remotely fancy about the Horsa; it was a basic, utilitarian troop-carrying glider, far less captivating than the sleek Mosquito. Yet the role played by the Horsa in the successful airborne landings on D-Day was equal to anything performed by others.

The Germans had pioneered the use of gliders during the Battle of France in 1940 when glider-borne paratroopers had swiftly captured the seemingly impregnable Belgium fortress of Eben-Emael. Landing silently within its walls, a few yards from their objective - huge guns within concrete casements - the defenders were taken by complete surprise. With easy access the guns were quickly destroyed and, demoralised by the speed of the action, the garrison surrendered.

Churchill was impressed, ordering that 'a parachute force numbering 5,000 men should be raised', and that force should include gliders.

By 1942 production of the Airspeed Horsa glider had swung into full operation. From the outset it was to be built almost entirely from pre-fabricated wooden parts. Factories that before the war had built furniture, staircases and window frames now turned their skills into building parts for gliders. Sub-contractors all over the country were soon delivering the parts to be assembled, skinned with plywood, and painted. Out of busy cocoons the new, snub-nosed gliders emerged, nearly 4,000 of them.

The Horsa - with its tricycle undercarriage and plump round fuselage slung beneath a huge wing - might have been basic, but it was utterly distinctive.

And impressive too: 67 ft long with an 80 ft wide wing that contained massive flaps and airbrakes powered by compressed air.

The fuselage itself, assembled from three basic sections, could be rapidly unbolted and taken apart when extracting loads of equipment in combat. The later MkII version was modified to include a hinged nose section to further ease unloading of heavy cargo, jeeps or light artillery.

Whereas the German gliders in Belgium had carried nine men, and the American WACO could cram 13 on board, the Horsa was in a different league altogether: it was big enough to embark an entire platoon of 28 paratroopers, plus its two-man crew. Used by both the British and Americans on D-Day, by the time all the extra equipment, ammunition and weapons had been loaded, the weight limits were tested to the extreme. The magnificent Horsas, however, shrugged concerns aside and, without effort, carried out their duties with flying colours.

Taken from an original drawing by Robert Taylor

WACO CG-4A
HADRIAN

Designed and built by the Waco Aircraft Company in Ohio and first flown in 1942, nearly 14,000 CG-4A gliders were built. It was the only US transport glider used operationally in combat by the Allies in Europe; the RAF, to be different, named it the 'Hadrian'.

It was much smaller than the Horsa but on D-Day this helped many of the pilots trying to land in the some of the smaller Normandy fields.

WACO gliders were used in all the major airborne operations in north-west Europe, as well in Burma where they supported General Orde Wingate's second Chindit operation in March 1944.

WACO - CRASH LANDING A detail from a painting by Robert Taylor

Original drawing by Richard Taylor

GENERAL AIRCRAFT
HAMILCAR Mk.I

It was a colossus, almost as big as the bomber that towed it. The biggest Allied glider of World War II, this mammoth creature was principally designed to carry a Tetrarch light-tank, the type used by the British 6th Airborne on D-Day.

The beast, with its hinged-nose ready for rapid unloading, could carry a staggering 17,500 lbs load and, in reality, was used to carry more than tanks. They could lift anti-tank guns, 25-pounder Howitzers, pairs of Bren Gun Carriers or Scout Cars - complete with their crews who sat in the vehicle throughout the flight. They could lift a bulldozer or carry large quantities of ammunition, medical or any other heavy supplies directly to the battle zone.

THE
GLIDER PILOT REGIMENT

'NIHIL IMPOSSIBILIS EST'

The men of the Glider Pilot Regiment were, perhaps, some of the least well-known yet most deserving heroes of World War II. Formed in 1942 entirely by volunteers from the Army, the regiment was unique; its men were not only trained as regular soldiers able to fight alongside the paratroops they carried, but all were skilful pilots. Their Regimental motto - *Nihil Impossibilis Est* or Nothing Is Impossible - was well suited to their task.

Nothing illustrated their courage and skill more than when, in the first few minutes of D-Day, glider pilots made possible the capture of the two bridges over the Orne. Landing perfectly in a moonlit field next to the Caen canal bridge, they brought their gliders in so accurately that they stopped just yards from their objective.

Staff Sergeant Jim Wallwork, already a veteran of Sicily, was the first pilot to land. As the glider slid to an abrupt stop, he was propelled head-first through the Perspex windscreen - unintentionally the first Allied soldier to set foot on French soil on D-Day!

Despite the blow, and with cuts to his head, he managed to drag his trapped co-pilot from the shattered cockpit and began to carry ammunition to the men on the bridge. For his superb feat of airmanship Wallwork was awarded the DFM.

'The pilots had done a fantastic job in bringing the slithering, bouncing and crippled glider to a halt with its nose buried into the canal bank and within seventy-five yards of the bridge. As I moved forward I glanced back towards the glider and saw that the entire front had been smashed inwards...'

Private Denis Edwards, D Company, 2nd Oxfordshire and Buckinghamshire Light Infantry.

The Devil's Own Luck by Denis Edwards.
Published by Pen & Sword Books.

Taken from an original drawing by Richard Taylor

An original drawing by Richard Taylor.

HAWKER
TYPHOON Mk.IV
THE REAPER OF FALAISE

Sidney Camm's immortal Hawker Hurricane had helped save Britain during the Battle of Britain. It was tough and reliable and in the early days of the war formed the backbone of Fighter Command. Hawker intended to replace it with a far superior machine, one that would be bigger, faster, more heavily armed and twice as powerful as the tried and trusted Hurricane.

On the drawing board the new interceptor, called the Typhoon, had looked like a winner; Hawker hoped it would become the best interceptor in the world. But now that it had been built, and flown, all was not well - in fact the project was turning into a disaster.

The problems were many: the newly developed and extremely powerful Napier Sabre engine was plagued with teething troubles. When it worked it worked well, but not for long. Most had to be completely overhauled after a couple of dozen hours. The drag caused by the new aircraft's thick wings blunted performance and, most dangerous of all, there were serious structural flaws; a prototype had already split almost in half during a mid-air test - the fact that the test pilot, Philip Lucas, managed to land was a miracle of flying, for which he was awarded the George Medal.

The Typhoon stood on the verge of cancellation. The fact that it was re-born was due mainly to a test pilot, a very young, but enthusiastic Flight Lieutenant called Roland 'Bee' Beamont.

RETURN OF THE HUNTERS by Anthony Saunders

Two RAF Typhoons from 245 Squadron, their rocket racks
empty after delivering a blistering strike against enemy
positions, pass over the American Mulberry Harbour off
Omaha beach as they race back to their base in Hampshire to
re-fuel and re-arm.

An original drawing by Richard Taylor.

'At first the Typhoon gave a lot of trouble - both the airframe and the engine - and we lost a lot of good pilots. However, once these faults were overcome, it became a very tough and reliable machine, and the very best gun platform. It carried bombs, rockets and, of course cannons and you could hold a steep dive far longer than the Me109 or Fw190. It could withstand high G-forces and its wide undercarriage was a great benefit to us on the rough airstrips in Normandy'.

Group Captain Denys Gillam, a former battle of Britain Spitfire Ace, who led 146 Typhoon Wing in Normandy in support of the Canadian Army.

The Military Gallery

Already a seasoned veteran with several victories to his credit - he had flown Hurricanes during the Battle of Britain - 'Bee' found himself in trouble with the authorities: in high spirits he had taken an attractive young WAAF up for a sight-seeing ride in his Hurricane. His CO was not amused and 'Bee' found himself court-martialled with a severe reprimand. He was sent off to Hawker as a Hurricane test pilot, but was soon working with Typhoons.

'Bee' was enthralled by the new machine, and later wrote:

"The Typhoon was tremendously impressive. At full throttle it showed more than 400 mph on the air speed indicator at low-level, and at 500mph reached in only a shallow dive, it was adequately controllable and stable, although extremely raucous. At more modest speeds it was very pleasantly manoeuvrable, and in particular it

showed exceptionally steady gun-aiming qualities in simulated attacks on ground-targets".

There now followed months of tough flight testing during which 'Bee' quickly concurred that the new aircraft was never going to make it as an all-out fighter. Its performance at high-altitude was lack-lustre, and the rear vision appalling. He did, however, recognise that the Typhoon could be developed into a magnificent low-level ground-attack fighter and was determined to prove it.

Flying over 50 combat missions, mainly at night, he set out to successfully attack a whole variety of ground targets. The results were impressive; he had proved his point and the Typhoon was back in favour.

'Bee' was posted to command 609 Typhoon Squadron, part of the new 2nd Tactical Air Force that contained every squadron that had been equipped with Typhoons. There now followed the first signs of the damage the Typhoons were later to exact in Normandy: devastating attacks on anything that moved. Trains, trucks and armoured vehicles, coastal shipping and E-boats, all came to fear the sound of approaching Typhoons. Airfields, bridges, supply dumps were targets too. In March 1944 'Bee' was promoted to command the, soon to be all Typhoon, 150 Wing. He was still only 23.

By D-Day there were 26 RAF, RCAF and RNZAF combat-ready Typhoon squadrons. They formed the backbone of the 2nd Tactical Air Force and were about to make up for all the trouble and heartbreak that had been caused in the early years of development.

No German soldier who heard the distinctive whine of the Typhoon's piston-engine, and survived, would ever forget the sound. For the others, however, it was one of the last sounds they heard. The Typhoon was both feared and hated in equal measure. Pilots who were shot down and captured could expect rough treatment.

Flight Lieutenant Roy Crane had a lucky escape. He was flying Typhoons with 181 Squadron, operating out of one of the new temporary airstrips. On 2 August he was attacking a column of tanks and vehicles near Falaise when his aircraft was hit by flak, forcing him to bale out. Unfortunately he landed in the middle of an SS encampment. Brutally man-handled, he was expecting summary execution when a senior Luftwaffe NCO and a colleague turned up from the flak position that had shot him down. A heated debate followed; Crane could only watch with horror as his fate was argued over. Luck, however, was on his side. His SS guard merely spat in his face before handing him over to the silver-tongued Luftwaffe man.

An original drawing by Richard Taylor.

THE CANADIANS original drawing by Richard Taylor

Johnnie Johnson and the Mk. IX Spitfires of his Canadian Wing

SUPERMARINE
SPITFIRE Mk.IX
FIGHTER SUPREME

RJMitchell would never have claimed to be a genius; he was a modest and retiring man. As head of design and aero-engineering at Supermarine, he shunned the limelight. But his quiet manner did indeed hide the talents of a genius, because R. J. Mitchell designed what was not only a supreme fighting machine, but the most beautiful aeroplane the world has ever seen - the Spitfire.

The sleek little fighter, with its elliptical wings and Merlin engine, flew like a dream and ever since that day in March 1936, when test pilot Matt Summers took the Spitfire up for the first time, both Supermarine and the Air Ministry knew they were on to a winner.

It was just as well, because the clouds of war were gathering over Europe. The first RAF Spitfires were entering service at the same time as Neville Chamberlain was stepping out of a BOAC Lockheed Electra at Heston aerodrome proclaiming 'peace in our time'. It wasn't to be; a year later Britain, and the Spitfire, found themselves at war.

There now started a never-ending battle for supremacy against its Luftwaffe counter-parts, a tussle that would see-saw throughout the war, first with the Bf109 and later the Focke-Wulf Fw190. Engines were improved and up-rated, cannons replaced machine-guns, wings were amended and propellers upgraded - anything to give that extra edge in a duel.

In the Battle of Britain it duelled equally with the Bf109 E but by 1941 it was the Spitfire Mk.V that ruled the skies, allowing the RAF to go on the offensive. Douglas Bader, who disliked the new cannons, flew one of the last Mk.Vs to be equipped solely with machine-guns. The introduction of the squat Focke-Wulf 190 with its big, powerful BMW engine tipped the scales towards

the Luftwaffe. The engineers at Rolls-Royce now had to squeeze every last ounce of power out of the Merlin for the Spitfire Mk.IX - by far the most numerous variant flying on D-Day.

On 6 June 1944, under grey, leaden skies, nine squadrons of Spitfires patrolled the beachhead, providing the fighter cover for the invasion beaches below. Many others kept watch over the sea-lanes and approaches. Seafires, drawn from the Royal Navy's Fleet Air Arm, and in liaison with the bombarding fleet, helped to direct fire from the huge naval guns on to their targets.

FIGHTER COVER by Robert Taylor

Original pencil drawing by Richard Taylor
Johnnie Johnson and Mk.IX Spitfires of his Canadian Wing,
June 1944

D-DAY SPITFIRE
Mk.IX

"During the Second War I flew Spitfire Mk. I, II, V, VI, IX and the XIV - the latter 'a nice first flying machine, but it's not a Spitfire any more' was my comment after my first flight in a Mk.XIV.....I preferred the trusty, graceful Spitfire Mk.IX - the best Spitfire of them all."

Air Vice Marshal Johnnie Johnson

The new Mk.IX had been a huge improvement on its Mk.V predecessor. With the new Merlin 61 engine it was considerably faster - topping out at 408 mph at 25,000 feet - and it could climb much higher to 43,000 feet, nearly 9,000 feet higher than before. It could also stay airborne for longer.

The Mk.IX was easy to spot: it had a longer, leaner nose, necessary to house the big Merlin 60-series engine, and stood very nearly three feet taller off the ground. A big, much-improved, four-bladed propeller was bolted on and, slung below the wing, a pair of large radiators.

On 10 June 1944, four days after the troops had hit the beaches, Spitfires flew into Sainte Croix-sur-Mer for the first time. They were the Mk.IXs from Johnnie Johnson's famous 144 Canadian Wing.

Flying from their base at Ford, on the Sussex coast near Tangmere, they touched down on French soil for just long enough to be quickly re-fuelled and re-armed before taking to the sky for their first combat sweep out of Normandy. An important milestone had been reached at the beginning of what Johnnie Johnson would later call their "exhilarating, buccaneering trek across France" when they finally moved further inland.

The outstanding Mk.IX continued to be built until the end of the war - 5,665 of them - even though the newer, more powerful, Griffon-engined Mk.XIV by then reigned supreme.

Sadly R.J. Mitchell never lived to see his beautiful little fighter become a legend. He never knew how much it contributed to the Allied victory; he died of illness in 1938. But even the modest Mitchell would surely have been moved to know the name he'd given it would be remembered for ever - Spitfire!

NORMANDY NEMESIS by Robert Taylor

Mk.IX Spitfires of 443 Squadron RCAF, based at Sainte Croix- sur- Mer, tangle with a group of Fw190s they had encountered on a fighter sweep near Alençon, on 23 June 1944. During the mêleé that followed, their Squadron Leader, Wally McLeod, quickly destroyed two Fw190s, whilst another Fw190 was badly damaged.

NORTH AMERICAN
P-51 MUSTANG
FINEST ESCORT OF THE WAR

WHERE EAGLES GATHERED by Robert Taylor

In the build up to D-Day, on 5 March 1944, B-24 Liberators of the 448th Bomb Group attacked a Luftwaffe base at Limoges in western France. But they ran into a bunch of Bf-109s from JG2. Luckily for the B-24s the P-51s of the 4th Fighter Group, Eighth Air Force, were on hand to send the attackers fleeing.

❝When I saw those Mustangs over Berlin, I knew the war was lost", Reichsmarshall Herman Goering is supposed to have said when P-51s first appeared in the skies over Berlin. Up till then, Berliners had got used to the sight of American bombers from whom, without an escort with the range to protect them, the Luftwaffe was exacting a terrible toll.

But then, in December 1943, a special Christmas present arrived for the hard-pressed bomber crews - the first P-51 Mustang appeared. With a far greater range than a P-47, the new Mustangs could now go all the way to Berlin, and back. Soon P-51s were streaming off the production lines and heading for Europe.

It had been inspired by the British - the aircraft conceived in the dark days of 1940 when Britain was desperate for fighters. North American had been building Harvard trainers for some time, and the RAF loved them. But could the company build them a first-class, single-seat fighter? North American's answer was immediate - yes - and just 120 days later the first P-51 made its maiden flight. It was a staggering achievement.

The British called it the Mustang and it was certainly quick - quick enough for the US military to take notice. And when, in 1942 a Rolls-Royce test pilot strapped one of their Merlin engines on board in place of its Allison, the Mustang was now the fastest kid on the block. The P-51 was a winner.

By 6 June 1944 there were thousands of P-51s for the Allies to call on. The sky was full of Mustangs. Many were escorting the bombers to and from strategic targets around the beaches, whilst others, such as the P-51 tactical elements within the US Ninth Air Force and the RAF's 2nd Tactical Air Force, supported the armies on the ground. For weeks after D-Day they continually harried, attacked and strafed any enemy target foolish enough to show itself.

On D-Day the mighty Mustang was way up there with the best.

DAWN BREAKERS by Anthony Saunders

P-51 Mustangs of the 359th Fighter Group, US Eighth Air Force, escort RAF Halifax bombers of 76 Squadron back across *Gold* beach following the dawn attack on the German battery at Mont Fleury. Far below them the first assault waves of the British 50th Division are storming ashore

HELL HAWKS OVER THE NORMANDY BRIDGEHEAD a drawing by Robert Taylor

P-47D Thunderbolts from the 365th Fighter Group, US Ninth Air Force - The Hell Hawks - head inland over the D-Day Normandy beaches in support of the US First Army. Flying from their base at Beaulieu in Hampshire, the 'Hell Hawks' successfully attacked and destroyed numerous strategic enemy positions behind the invasion bridgehead.

REPUBLIC
P-47 THUNDERBOLT
THE JUG

When the former Eagle Squadron pilots of the 4th Fighter Group got their first look at a Thunderbolt they were staggered by the sheer size of the thing in front of them. It was a juggernaut, and a clumsy-looking one at that.

Dominated by a giant 2,000 horsepower, gas-guzzling Pratt & Witney radial engine up front, a big four-bladed propeller and tubby round fuselage, the jumbo leviathan towered over everyone gathered around on the hard-standing. Their shock was perhaps understandable because, up till now, these particular pilots had been flying the sleekest fighter of them all - the Spitfire.

Eyes widened as the first of them climbed up to inspect the cockpit. Compared to their Spitfires there was so much room, in fact there was more room than in any other fighter. RAF pilots later quipped that if P-47 pilots wanted to avoid enemy fire, all they had to do was run around in the cockpit!

Once in the air, however, even the most sceptical were won over. The great strength of the Thunderbolt was its ability to take punishment and get you home, no matter how badly you'd been shot up, earning everlasting respect from the pilots who flew them. A saying went along the lines of - if you wanted to impress a girl back home, you flew a P-51. But, if you wanted to get back to the girl back home, you flew a P-47 Thunderbolt.

More Thunderbolts were built than any other US fighter during the war and, armed with eight .5-inch Browning machine-guns, they packed a deadly punch. P-47s shot down more enemy aircraft in aerial combat than any other Allied fighter. They also flew more sorties than those of the P-51 and P-38 combined.

Only the 56th Fighter Group, the one that had been the first to receive the P-47, held on to their mounts till the end of the war.

By D-Day, with the arrival of the long-range P-51, most P-47s had transitioned from high-altitude escort fighter to probably the most effective American fighter-bomber of the entire war. And in Normandy, more than anywhere else, their reputation as such was fully cemented. In the weeks following D-Day the P-47s went on the rampage.

Equipped with armour-piercing bullets that smashed their way through all but the heavily armoured tanks, a P-47's Browning machine-guns could tear through anything unlucky enough to be in its way. P-47s shot up

BRIDGE BUSTERS by Anthony Saunders

P-47 Thunderbolts from the 78th Fighter Group launch a blistering low-level attack on a German train attempting to re-supply their army in Normandy, June 1944.

THUNDERBOLT STRIKE by Robert Taylor

P-47 Thunderbolts of the 404th Fighter group, US Ninth Air force, clear the target area after a low-level attack on the airfield inland from Le Havre, Normandy, 1944. Tracer winds up towards them from ground defences and almost all the aircraft have taken hits. Ground-attack pilots went in low, did the job and got out fast!

MIGHTY EIGHTH - OUTWARD BOUND
by Robert Taylor

From April 1943 until October 1945 the historic RAF Duxford was home to the famous 78th Fighter Group, US Eighth Air Force. Shortly after D-Day, their P-47s with invasion stripes hastily applied, they prepare to embark on another escort mission. Overhead, a flight of P-51s from a nearby base head out too.

trains, strafed airfields, and within a matter of minutes could transform a convoy of vehicles into nothing more than a line of battered burning metal.

They carried a hefty bomb load, too - even greater than that of the Luftwaffe's Dornier Do17 bombers that had blitzed London in 1940. And in June and July 1944 the P-47s used that capacity to the full. They bombed bridges, viaducts, railway lines, junctions, artillery and tanks. Anything that helped the Germans could expect a visit from a P-47.

Original pencil drawing by Richard Taylor

THE LONG SHORT DAYS by Robert Taylor

Bf109Gs from III./JG26 return to their forward base in
northern France after a long fighter sweep along the
Channel coast in early 1944.

MESSERSCHMITT
Bf 109 G

It was the backbone of the Luftwaffe. At some point in their career almost every German pilot had flown it. It was credited with more victories than any other fighter in the history of air combat and was built in greater numbers than any other fighter. It was, by far, the longest serving German interceptor, and became the cornerstone on which Hitler's Luftwaffe was formed. Its name was very simple - Bf109.

The history of the Bf109 went back a long way, to March 1934 when Willi Messerschmitt, then Chief Designer at Bayerische Flugzeugwerke - Bavarian Aircraft Works - sat down at his drawing board to start work on a new, single-seat, monoplane interceptor. He was determined to win the prize to build the Luftwaffe's new interceptor.

His plans were radical. The new airframe and fuselage would be all-metal, not a hint of fabric in sight. The cockpit would be enclosed for all weathers and, unlike others, it would have a retractable undercarriage for greater streamlining and speed. The new design was given the designation Bf109 and took its first flight in May 1935.

The Luftwaffe loved the Bf109, and bought it. From that moment on the words Luftwaffe and Bf109 became synonymous.

In 1938 the Bayerische Flugzeugwerke transformed itself into a new and bigger company, named after its new Chairman - Messerschmitt. From then on all new aircraft designs were to be labelled Me, with only those already in existence retaining the Bf designation.

At the outbreak of way, the Luftwaffe had one distinct edge over the RAF - many of their top commanders had battlefield experience. They had flown the Bf109 in combat with the Condor Legion in 1937 during the Spanish Civil War, and knew their aircraft backwards. The RAF had to learn quickly, the hard way.

For the Bf109 there now began a five-and-half year battle with its arch nemesis - the Spitfire. From the battle for France, through the Battle of Britain and the sparring years thereafter, the two aircraft jousted for superiority. By June 1944 the Bf109 G version, introduced in 1942, was still bearing the brunt of the fighting and, with many improvements, would continue to do so till the end of the war. More Bf109Gs were built than any other type and it

was now playing numerous roles, in every combat theatre that the Luftwaffe was involved in. Escort, interceptor, night-fighter, fighter-bomber and ground attack - the Bf109 was supposed to do them all. But the tide of war was against it.

On D-Day the Allied air forces could call on 11,590 aircraft to support the landings in Normandy. In the whole of France the Luftwaffe could muster only a fraction of that number, some of which were Bf109s. Whilst the Allies flew 14,674 sorties on 6 June, the Luftwaffe put up a little more than 300. They were hopelessly under-strength and undermanned. Few of the great Aces who had duelled with the RAF in the earlier years had survived, and of those that had, most were hard-pressed away on the Eastern Front. In France the Luftwaffe's ranks had been weakened by a lack of training as new pilots were rushed through instruction and straight to the Front. For the Luftwaffe, and for the Bf109, the end was in sight.

LOCKHEED
P-38 LIGHTNING
THE FORK-TAILED DEVIL

"The sweetest-flying plane in the sky" General Jimmy Doolittle

DOOLITTLE'S D-DAY by Robert Taylor

Never one to shirk from excitement, General Jimmy Dolittle, Commander of the US Eighth Air Force, took off in the early moments of D-Day to see for himself how the landings were going. He was able to give General Eisenhower the first eyewitness report of the fighting.

The Luftwaffe called the hard-hitting, twin-boom P-38 fighter - *der Gabelschwanz-Teufel* - the fork-tailed devil. Everyone else called it the Lightning. Overshadowed by the mighty Mustang and the tough P-47, the P-38 Lightning was probably the most under-valued American fighter in Europe.

The P-38 was, however, a stalwart. They were in action from the moment the Eighth Air Force first arrived in Britain. On Friday 14 August 1942, a P-38 from the 27th Fighter Squadron, transitioning through Iceland, shared in the destruction of a Focke-Wulf 200 Condor.

It was the first German aircraft to be shot down by the Americans in World War II.

Although it had a better range than the P-47, the Lightning was still no match for the P-51 when it came to escorting the big bombers. But, by the time the P-51s arrived to replace them, the P-38 was getting quite a reputation for itself in another role - ground attack.

Returning from escort duties P-38s had always had success shooting up targets of opportunity. Now, with D-Day approaching, the P-38s were fully unleashed on ground attack, and then, in Normandy, to tactical support. They bombed and strafed railways, supply depots, airfields, armour and columns of enemy troops. They even had the cheek to attack Generalfeldmarschall von Kluge's headquarters.

As the Allied armies pushed rapidly west, and operating from airfields in France, P-38s struck ever deeper behind the fast-retreating enemy lines. Nothing in the Reich was now safe from Lockheed's adaptable 'fork-tailed devil'.

TACTICAL SUPPORT by Richard Taylor

A pair of Lockheed P-38 Lightnings streak over the recently liberated Pegasus Bridge shortly after D-Day in support of Allies battling against heavy German armour at the front. Below, signs of the recent action are still plainly visible as trucks and their exhausted drivers hasten back to the beachhead to collect reinforcements.

HAWKER
TEMPEST Mk.V
THE BEST LOW-LEVEL FIGHTER OF THE WAR

TEMPESTS OVER MONT SAINT MICHEL

An original drawing by Richard Taylor

Tempests overfly Mont Saint Michel lying just off the French coast near Avranches. Dominated by the ancient abbey and monastery, the formidable site had been fortified for centuries. It is one of the most recognisable sites in Europe.

If 'Bee' Beamont had played a significant part in the survival, and eventual success, of the Typhoon programme, he played an even bigger role in ensuring that the follow-up was a winner from the start.

He later wrote: "As a direct result of the Typhoon trials, Hawkers were able to incorporate significant improvements in a Typhoon Mk.II development - later named Tempest - and in late 1943 I was posted back to the factory to test the new version with a thinner wing, more fuel, improved 'spring-tab' ailerons for high-rolling

power at the approved dive speed of 545 mph and, most impressively, a completely redesigned windscreen and all-round 'rear vision' canopy.

"This proved to be the first general-purpose fighter for low-altitude war of 1944; and, after an exciting five months of testing the Tempest at the Langley factory, I was again privileged to take this new fighter into action for the first time, in 150 Wing at Newchurch from May 1944 onwards.

"We scored the Tempest's first ground-attack success in the softening up period prior to D-day in June and shot down some Bf109Gs, over Rouen two days after D-Day".

Shortly after D-Day, on 13 June, the game-plan changed - the Germans launched the first of Hitler's new 'miracle weapons'. Four V-1 'doodle-bug' flying bombs sped through anti-aircraft fire towards southern England. Two days later, things got worse when 73 V-1s fell on London.

The Tempest, together with the new Spitfire Mk.XIV and Mustang Mk.III, was one of the few Allied aircraft with the speed to catch the new rocket-propelled flying bombs. 'Bee' and his Wing were sent out to help stop them. By the end of August, 632 'doodle-bugs' had been destroyed by the Tempests, either by shooting them down or 'tip-tripping' them over the Channel - flicking the flying bomb's wing up with their own, toppling it over into the sea below.

ANOTHER ONE FOR THE BAG
An original pencil drawing by Robert Taylor

A Hawker Tempest from 3 Squadron, Newchurch Wing, tip-tripping an inbound V-1 flying-bomb heading for London.

'DINAH MIGHT' by Anthony Saunders (detail)

A detail taken from the original painting UTAH DAWN highlights the B-26 Marauder 'Dinah Might' flown by Major David H. Dewhurst of the 386th Bomb Group as they head over *Utah* Beach to attack the coastal gun batteries.

MARTIN
B-26 MARAUDER

The 'honour' of first combat on D-Day fell not to a Spitfire, Mustang or Typhoon, but to the Martin B-26 Marauder, It was a medium bomber. At 05.20 hours a gaggle of Fw190s from III./JG2 briefly engaged B-26s over the Pointe du Hoc. One Fw190 was shot down in the clash.

The Marauder wasn't the easiest of aircraft to fly; it took plenty of pilot experience to handle some of its trickier characteristics. But, once mastered, Martin's B-26 proved itself a potent and reliable operator with an impressive war record: at one point there were nearly 2,000 of them operating in Europe and, by the end of hostilities, the B-26 had an overall loss rate in combat of less than one per cent. This was the lowest of any aircraft in the USAAF.

By 6 June 1944 the US Ninth Air Force had evolved into one of the largest tactical air forces the world has ever seen, and the B-26 Marauder was its medium bomber of choice. Operating with fighter escort at medium altitude, it was used extensively not only on D-Day but throughout the battle for Normandy and the advance into Germany. By which time the underestimated Marauder had gained the reputation of being one of the most valuable and accurate medium bombers of the entire war.

By the time the last B-26 entered service, more than 5,100 aircraft had flowed off Martin's production lines in Baltimore, Maryland and *Omaha*, Nebraska. The thousands of men and women who built them could take great pride in what they had helped to create - the B-26 Marauder - one of the great 'unsung' heroes of World War II.

MARAUDER MISSION by Robert Taylor

B-26 Marauders of the 386th Bomb Group, US Ninth Air Force, return from attacking targets in the Pas de Calais in the months before D-Day. By May 1944, the Ninth Air Force was despatching more than one thousand aircraft a day against targets in Normandy and the Pas de Calais.

FOCKE-WULF
Fw 190A

PREPARING THE WOLVES by Richard Taylor

Ground crew of 9./JG-2 make final adjustments and re-arm their Fw-190s at an airfield near the ancient walled city of Vannes in Brittany. The airfield was overrun by American forces during the first week of August 1944.

Oberstleutnant 'Pips' Priller had been woken at dawn: there were reports of Allied landings west of Caen. He was Kommodore of JG-26, and at 08.00 hours he and his wingman lifted off from their airfield outside Lille and banked their Fw190s south-west to investigate.

Quite how they made it unnoticed through the protecting fighter screen no one knows but, as they approached the coast, the sight that greeted them was unbelievable - the beaches below were black with men and armour, the sea a mass of craft. He knew immediately that this was the invasion they'd all been waiting for.

The two airmen were low on fuel but, still blinking in disbelief, they just had time to turn their Fw190A-8s into a steep banking dive and make a single strafing pass along the beach known to the Allies as *Sword*. It was one of the precious few sorties the Luftwaffe made that day.

The fact that it was a pair of Fw190s to break through was fitting because, when they had first appeared in the skies of France, no-one in RAF Intelligence had taken the squat-looking fighter seriously. How could it possibly have the measure of their elegant Spitfire Mk.Vs?

They had under-estimated it as top pilot Johnnie Johnson soon found out: "This splendid fighter - the redoubtable Focke-Wulf Fw190 - with its high speed, good ceiling, and four 20mm cannon completely out-classed our Spitfire Mk.Vs to such an extent that,

although we restricted our offensive missions, our casualties increased".

The Fw190 dominated the skies of the Western Front until the new Spitfire Mk.IX could finally restore equality.

"It was a wonderful aircraft. I could turn it on a plate, the wings being white from condensation and to pull it out of a dive at 440mph was no problem. The Bf109 wasn't strong enough to do that. Against the British, our aircraft were so well matched that it all came down to the skill of the pilot."

Luftwaffe Ace Major Erich Rudorffer, 224 victories and holder of the Knight's Cross, Oak Leaves and Swords.

BREAKING COVER by Robert Taylor

Concealed under the cover of trees from the prying eyes of Allied fighters, Fw 190 pilots
break cover from in a wood in northern France, ready for a quick take-off.

AVRO
LANCASTER
COLOSSUS OF BOMBER COMMAND

There can be no doubt that the Avro Lancaster was the RAF's greatest - and most famous - bomber of World War II. Developed out of the under-powered and unreliable twin-engined Manchester, the Lancaster, with its four Merlin engines, was the complete opposite. Reliable, strong, a joy to fly, it could carry a huge bomb load that included the whopping 22,000 lb 'Grand Slam' bomb. From the moment it entered service in early 1942 the Lancaster was the rock upon which Bomber Command then formed.

In the early hours of D-Day, Lancasters had been among the hundreds of others pounding German defences in Normandy. At the same time 617 Squadron, of Dambuster fame, was engaged in *Operation Taxable* which, in conjunction with *Operation Glimmer*, involved the precision dropping of 'window' or 'chaff' - thin strips of metal - designed to confuse German radar operators into thinking that an invasion fleet was steaming towards them. Whilst *Glimmer* headed for the Pas de Calais, 617 Squadron's Lancasters and *Taxable* were aiming for the Cap d'Antifer, twelve miles north of Le Havre.

On 18 July Lancasters formed a large part of the 1,570 strong bomber force that dropped nearly 8,000 tons of bombs on German positions just before *Operation Goodwood* - the British and Canadian thrust south of Caen. On 25 July they were on hand to support the US First Army during *Operation Cobra* - the start of the break-out from Normandy.

Throughout the entire Normandy campaign, however, the Lancasters of Bomber Command carried on with the task of systematically destroying Germany's capacity to wage war. Night after night, in ever-increasing formations, they headed for the industrial cities of the Reich tasked with the eradication of aircraft assembly lines, tank plants, truck production, factories, engineering works and steel mills. This crescendo of bombing left the German forces in Normandy short of aircraft, armour, ammunition and equipment. And for that, the magnificent Lancaster must take much of the credit.

DAY DUTIES FOR THE NIGHT WORKERS by Robert Taylor
Ground crew prepare the massive Lancaster for the coming night's action. There are engines to be checked over, guns to be armed, bombs to be loaded and near-empty fuel tanks to be filled.

LAST FLIGHT HOME by Robert Taylor

As the harvesting proceeds below, the last flight of
Lancasters thunders home after another tough daylight raid
on German positions shortly after D-Day. With gear down,
the weary crews make their final approach to landing, and a
brief, but well-earned, rest.

THE COST OF VICTORY

The battle to liberate Normandy came at a high cost: by the end more than 425,000 Allied and German soldiers had either been killed, wounded or were missing, their bodies never recovered. For the soldiers fighting on the ground the battle had claimed the lives of nearly 37,000 men. Over 16,000 serving with the Allied air forces had also died.

On D-Day itself the number of casualties is generally thought to have been around 10,000. That figure includes 2,500 killed, with the heaviest price being paid by those on *Omaha*. As high as the casualty figures were, they were far less than many had feared.

In the Battle of Normandy it might be easy to overlook the suffering of the French civilians: in excess of 15,000 had been killed.

Original pencil drawing by Richard Taylor

DINAH MIGHT by Anthony Saunders

B-26 *Dinah Might* and Marauders of the 386th Bomb Group, US Ninth Air Force, with freshly-applied invasion markings are escorted by P-51Bs on 6 June 1944. Despite the initial sluggish response from Luftwaffe fighters, casualty figures in the air battle steadily mounted in the weeks after D-Day, resulting in large part from the barrage of intense flak that greeted almost every bomber raid. Between 6 June and 30 June the Allied air forces lost more than 1,200 aircraft over the fighting in France, of which over 300 came from the Ninth Air Force.

Original pencil drawing by Richard Taylor

ACKNOWLEDGEMENTS

We wish to thank the D-Day Museum, Portsmouth for their kind permission to reproduce many of the quotations used in this book, and for the source material from which much of this text has been drawn.

Portsmouth's D-Day Museum is the only one in Britain dedicated solely to covering all aspects of the D-Day landings in Normandy.

All other permissions are courtesy of the Military Gallery, or as cited.

FURTHER BIBLIOGRAPHY:

Anthony Beevor: D-Day - The Battle for Normandy (Penguin Books 2012)

Ken Ford and Steven J. Zaloga: Overlord - The Illustrated History of the D-Day Landings (Osprey 2009)

Lloyd Clark: D-Day Pegasus - The Red Devils in Normandy (The History Press 2012)

Sir Winston Churchill: The Second World War / Hinge of Fate (The Reprint Society 1953)

William Jordan: The Normandy Mulberry Harbours (Pitkin 2012)

Martin Evans and William Jordan: D-day and the Battle of Normandy (Pitkin 2013)

Robert M. Pierce: Airborne Field Artillery: from inception to combat operations (Cameron University, Oklahoma, 1985)

www.history.army.mil/documents/WWII

www.coppheroes.org

www.pegasusarchive.org

www.greenhowards.org.uk

www.thinkdefence.co.uk/little known story of Percy Hobart

www.6juin1944.com